COOK'S TOURS
THE STORY OF POPULAR TRAVEL

EDMUND SWINGLEHURST

COOK'S TOURS presents a light-hearted but complete and informational picture of the evolution of popular travel from 1850 to the present day. It shows how the marketing of travel in the early days of exhortation of workers to claim their right to holidays has progressed to today's sophisticated promotion of the temptations of foreign holidays. It also examines the business aspects of travel from its beginnings in the hands of enthusiastic amateurs to its present-day status as an industry attracting the financial backing of banks and business houses and the support of governments.

Developments in popular travel and social attitudes towards the whole business of leisure travel and travellers are revealed not only in what was written contemporaneously, but also in the styles of approach in advertising ephemera, pamphlets of advice to travellers, music-hall songs, cartoons and the journals the travellers themselves kept.

Posters, brochures, travel magazines and photographs show the development of mass travel and its effect on politics, women's emancipation, social manners and morality in Britain and (because the British introduced tourism to the world) abroad. Edmund Swinglehurst has gathered his copious illustration material from the archives of rail, steamship and air companies and travel agencies and, in particular, from the extensive archives of the Thomas Cook Collection and of the Wagons-Lits Company. He lets the visual material speak for itself, while providing plenty of signposts to its essential significance.

Among the twenty books they have published are the *Victorian and Edwardian Seaside, Romantic Journey* and *Walks and Legends in Scotland*.

Mr Swinglehurst has four children, ranging in age from 40 to 3, and two grandchildren.

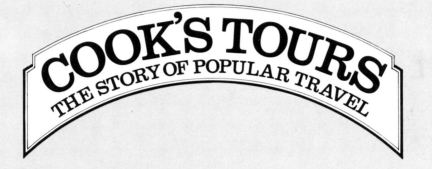

COOK'S TOURS
THE STORY OF POPULAR TRAVEL

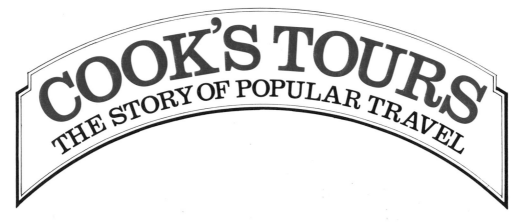

COOK'S TOURS
THE STORY OF POPULAR TRAVEL

EDMUND SWINGLEHURST

BLANDFORD PRESS
Poole   Dorset

First published in the U.K. 1982 by Blandford Press,
Link House, West Street, Poole, Dorset, BH15 1LL,
in association with Limelight Ltd, Halfpenny Green,
Chudleigh Knighton, Devon TQ13 0HD.

Distributed in the United States by
Sterling Publishing Co., Inc.,
2 Park Avenue, New York, N.Y. 10016.

British Library Cataloguing in Publication Data

Swinglehurst, Edmund
  Cook's Tours.
  1. Thomas Cook and Son—History
  2. Travel agents—Great Britain—History
  338.7'6191   G154

ISBN 0 7137 1183 3

Designed by Vic Giolitto
Typeset by Keyspools Ltd, Golborne, Lancashire
Printed by Tonbridge Printers Ltd.

Contents

CHAPTER ONE

Worker's Playtime

There was a clashing of cast-iron buffers, the thin wail of a whistle, the huffing and puffing of a steam engine, the blare of a brass band, the roar of a crowd of two thousand people, and Mr Thomas Cook's first excursion train moved slowly out of Leicester station. It was 5 July 1841 and the work of months as well as the career of the secretary of the Leicester Temperance Society were assured at last.

Thomas Cook was thirty-three at the time, a dark-haired, balding man who, since he had started work at the age of ten, had tried his hand at market gardening, preaching, cabinet making, printing and clerical work. In 1841 he had become the secretary of the Leicester Temperance Society, a job which was only as secure as the funds of the Society permitted but which he needed desperately to fulfil his responsibilities as a married man and father of a two-year-old son.

Writing in later years, Cook liked to indulge his tendency to dramatise events by describing the moment when he thought of running excursions as a 'revelation'. The road from Market Harborough, the centre of the Midland Temperance movement and the village where Cook lived, to Leicester, where he was bound for a temperance meeting, was his road to Damascus.

'About midway between Harborough and Leicester,' he wrote some years later, 'a thought flashed through my brain—what a glorious thing it would be if the newly developed power of steam railways and locomotion could be made subservient to the promotion of Temperance.'

To the dispassionate biographer looking back over Cook's life and career, it seems more likely that Cook had for some time been turning over in his mind the tenuous fortunes of his Leicester Temperance Society and considering how they and his own job could be buttressed against collapse.

Cook was an observant man, gregarious and talkative, and during his stint as a preacher, when he travelled over two thousand miles a year in the Midlands—most of it on foot—he must have become aware of the thoughts and feelings of people all over the country. Like Cobbett, he was an itinerant observer who drew conclusions from what he saw. The strains and stresses of the adjustment to an industrial and urban way of life for a population hitherto agricultural, cannot have escaped his notice. The vice and violence that this created was certainly in his mind, as his interest in religion and Temperance demonstrates. He was therefore mentally poised to take advantage of some opportunity to act for his ideals and at the same time for the well-being of his family. These two motives were brought together in the enterprise that was born with his first excursion.

Right from the start, Cook showed the qualities that enabled him to become the unrivalled master of the new business of cheap travel. First he had to persuade the Temperance Society to launch itself into the business of organised outings, then to convince the Midland Counties Railway Company that his was a viable scheme. The

Cheap railway travel in the mid-nineteenth century was provided in open trucks and passengers risked being burnt by sparks from the engine and injuries caused by derailment. This illustration shows the cover of a songsheet *c.* 1880.

THE EXCURSION TRAIN GALOP

BY

FRANK MUSGRAVE.

LONDON BOOSEY & SONS 24 & 28 HOLLES STREET

former he did by an eloquent appeal to the Society to approve the charter of a special train to carry friends of Temperance from Leicester to Loughborough for a meeting in support of the cause. This was the easiest of his tasks; getting the railways to cooperate with him was more difficult. They had no idea who he was, nor had they any reason to suppose that he could fill their empty seats better than they could themselves.

Cook arranged a meeting with John Fox Bell, secretary of the Midland Counties Railway, and put to him a proposition slightly different from the one he had made to

the Leicester Temperance Society. He knew that as a newly established railway the Midland Counties was having difficulty in finding passengers, for in common with all the railways it had to overcome public prejudice about riding around on what many people regarded as a dangerous form of transport. In addition to this, the cost of travel was too high for most people as it was based on the fares of stagecoaches which held only a few people, while railways could, and needed to, carry many score.

As a secretary of the Leicester Temperance Society, he had contacts all over the Midlands including in such large towns as Derby and Nottingham and could therefore guarantee to find enough passengers from all these areas for the Temperance excursion to Leicester; moreover, in order to attract the largest possible number of people, he would arrange a Gala at the park owned by an affluent member of the Temperance Society who lived in Loughborough.

What Cook offered to the Midland Counties Railway was not an appeal to charity and doing good work but a business offer. If Midland chartered him a train at a reasonable price, he would fill it.

Mr Bell was impressed, so much so that he even advanced Cook some money for promoting the venture. It was now up to Cook to prove to his backers that they were on to a winner.

For the next few weeks, Cook must have survived on very little sleep. When he was not travelling to the Midlands cities and persuading their Temperance Societies to join in his excursion, he was putting up posters at dead of night, on every available wall and fence in the region. He made his arrangements for entertainments at Mr Paget's Park, hired a brass band, distributed leaflets—and prayed.

The Illustrated London News artist sketched this impression of excursionists waiting for a train (*c.* 1880).

Letters from the sea: while Thomas Cook was conducting his first tour round the world in 1872–3 he wrote reports for *The Times*. Jules Verne's *Round the World in Eighty Days* was being serialised in a Paris newspaper at the time.

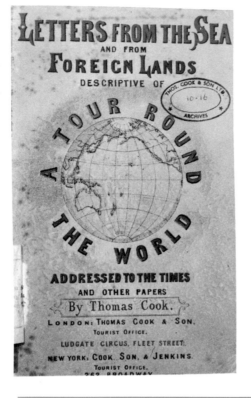

OPPOSITE
Cook's Excursionist, the newspaper started by Thomas Cook to stimulate travel to the Great Exhibition. The very first issue was actually called *The Exhibition Herald* (c. 1880).

Cook's Continental Railway Timetable was first published in 1873. Today it has a companion volume which gives times of trains all over the world.

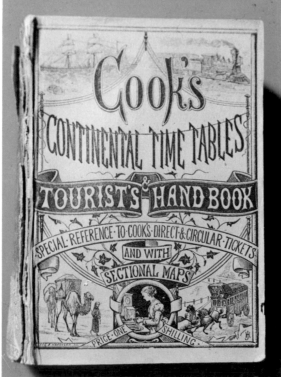

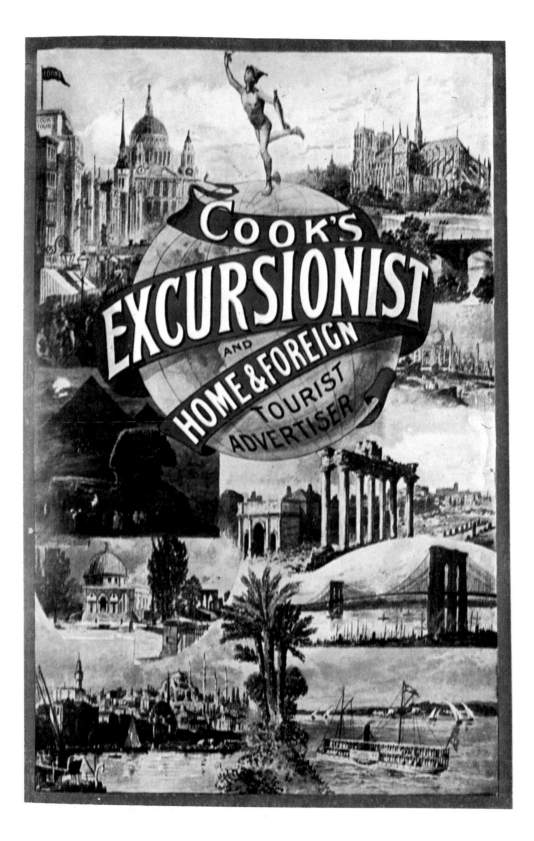

On receiving a concession enabling him to offer a cheap excursion fare to the Great Exhibition of 1851, Thomas Cook began to publish his *Excursionist and Exhibition Advertiser*. This is a later issue of 1862, promoting the Paris Exhibition.

The first excursion run by Thomas Cook for his personal profit was to Liverpool, in 1845. He published a special handbook which gave details of the trip and the places to be visited.

The success of the first Thomas Cook conducted excursion is recorded for posterity in the *Leicester Chronicle*. At the end of the day over two thousand people had turned up at Loughborough, only six hundred of them managing to squash themselves into the open trucks of the train. One thousand of them had been fed on tea and ham loaves, some had played cricket, others kiss-in-the-ring, and many had listened to the impassioned speeches from the Temperance platform. As the day drew to an end, a suspicion grew that the red, overheated glow clearly in evidence on many faces had been caused, not by exertion or excitement, but by the very demon drink that the outing had been designed to attack.

Thus, right from the start, the Cook's Tour was an exuberant blend of many aspects of social life and a mixture of that business flair and idealism that Victorians and Edwardians found easy to understand and to support.

The Midland was the first railway company to co-operate with Cook in his cheap excursion ticket schemes, and by 1904 its network had spread far and wide.

The success of the excursion arranged for the Leicester Temperance Society did not immediately change the fortunes of the organization and to raise money Cook was obliged to sell at half price many of the publications and tracts produced at his print works, on the sale of which he depended for his living.

Cook decided to move from Market Harborough to Leicester, hoping that in the larger town he could set himself up full-time as a printer. There are no records to indicate what happened in the next few years, though we know that Cook was much sought after to arrange excursions for Temperance Societies and Sunday Schools. Two events seem to indicate that the move to Leicester was a wise one. One was that funds were raised for the building of a Temperance Hall in Leicester itself and the other that Cook received the printer's contract for the production of the tracts and leaflets required by the Society. To make doubly sure that money would not be

Following the success of his Liverpool trip Cook immediately decided to arrange excursions to Scotland—the holiday home of Queen Victoria and Albert. This brochure, published in 1900, shows the continued popularity of tours north of the border.

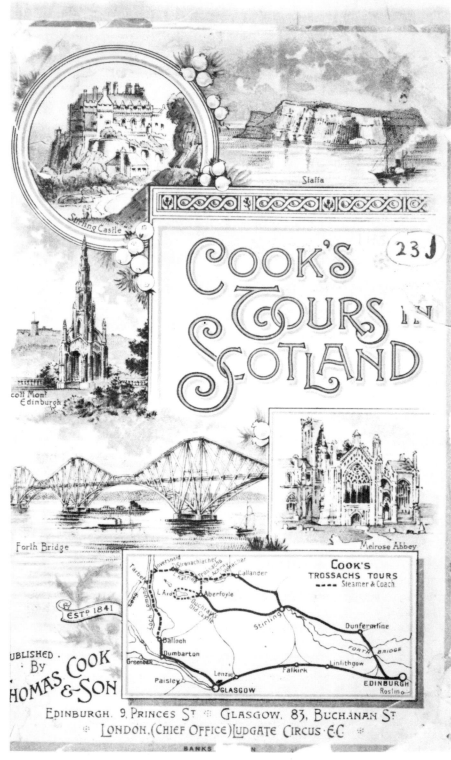

BELOW
A visit to the gardens of Coleorton Hall was included in this excursion to Ashby-de-la-Zouch and visitors were expressly asked not to pluck flowers or handle the statues (1850).

The seaside provided new opportunities for Cook's excursion ticket system. Scarborough offered steamboat trips as well as two mineral springs and bathing (1859).

short, Cook opened a Temperance Hotel which his wife Marianne was to manage.

At this point, one can discern in Thomas Cook the transformation of the dreamy idealist floating from job to job into a man who had become persuaded of his mission in life and was beginning to marshal the resources he needed to achieve it. 'Travel for the millions' changes from a rhetorical phrase to a precise target.

In 1845 Thomas Cook made a fateful decision. He would no longer organize tours just for the temperance societies but as a commercial business. His first venture was a Cook's Tour to Liverpool, at that time the glamorous gateway to North Wales and North America.

This time Cook was on his own, for although he had the contacts made during the years of his association with the Leicester Temperance Society, he could not take their support for granted. He had to sell his tour to the public on the strength of its interest, its value and the standing of his own name.

Cook worked like a demon to ensure that everything would go well. He persuaded the four railway companies that would be involved in transporting his passengers to grant him special coaches at a reduced price; he personally visited

Liverpool, examining the hotels and restaurants that could be recommended to his customers; he arranged side tours to Caernarvon and Snowdon; he wrote a guide book and, as with the first excursion, printed, distributed and posted all the advertising material himself, though he was no doubt helped by his son John Mason Cook, now a lad of eleven.

This first excursion in private enterprise proved an immediate success. All the fourteen-shilling first class and ten-shilling second class tickets sold out and were even resold on the black market. Altogether, some three hundred and fifty people arrived in Caernarvon that summer's day in 1845, and they were escorted around the town and castle by an English-speaking Welsh guide specially hired for the occasion. A fortnight later Cook repeated the tour and on this occasion accompanied the party that walked up Snowdon. While there, staring out over the beautiful Welsh mountains, he had his second revelation, as he put it when he wrote about it years later: he knew that his next move had to be to Scotland.

If his decision had been reached through calculated reasoning and not, as Cook claimed, through inspiration, it could not have been a better one. Scotland was the newly discovered holiday home of Queen Victoria and her beloved Albert. Romanticism in literature had made wild glens, blasted moorlands, overgrown gardens, grottoes, ruined castles and stormy skies the landscape of the early Victorian soul. It suited the reaction against the industrial prison that was growing around the nation and it expressed the nostalgia for an idealised natural world that Rousseau had first given voice to in France.

Like his contemporaries, Cook was not consciously aware of the reasons for the romantic trend but he did know, instinctively, that Scotland was a promising area for his tours.

There were difficulties. There was as yet no railway line across the border and the Tyne and Leith Steamship Company which could have taken his passengers up the coast to Edinburgh from Newcastle, the northern terminus of the railways, would have nothing to do with him. Undeterred, Cook made arrangements for a west coast tour from Leicester to Fleetwood, then by steamer to Ardrossan and by rail to Glasgow. From there another railway company would take the party on to Edinburgh. He offered the whole tour, personally conducted by himself, for one guinea and got three hundred and fifty customers.

It was not the first nor the last time that Cook answered a rebuff by finding an alternative route. Throughout his life, he was up against those who resisted innovation and who saw in his success a threat to their own rigid ways of doing business.

The arrival in Glasgow in 1846 was a triumph he was to repeat many times over during the next ten years as he expanded his tours to more and more parts of Britain. In a country where the population consisted of small communities that had little contact with each other, the appearance of groups of tourists who had come from hundreds of miles away was amazing, and the citizens of the towns visited would show their astonishment and excitement by turning out in force to see the Cook tourists; waving flags, firing off cannons and playing them in with the local brass band.

Such spectacles as those which greeted the Cook's Tours are never likely to be witnessed again, unless we are visited by beings from outer space, and they generated a curiosity and excitement about travel that soon swept through the whole nation.

'Cook's Excursion'—the cover of one of
many song sheets celebrating Cook's
Tours (c. 1900).

OPPOSITE
'Cook's Excursion Gallop'—the cover of
a song sheet which describes tourists
visiting Vesuvius. The bearded figure in
the centre is John Mason Cook, son of
Thomas (c. 1900).

CHAPTER TWO

Moving On

The early excursions to Liverpool and Scotland were only spare-time activities carried out during the summer months, and Thomas Cook's main business continued to be that of printing. Since he had taken over the Temperance Society Tract repository and set up his own printing press—from which he poured out such publications as *The Temperance Messenger*, *The Childrens Temperance Magazine*, *The Anti-Smoker* and *Progressive Temperance Reformer*—Thomas Cook had been considering ways of expanding his seasonal excursion business.

He was helped by two factors: one was the increasing competition among the railway companies, which were proliferating all over the country and looking for ways in which to increase their traffic; the other was a growing desire among the people for leisure and knowledge. Travel provided both and therefore satisfied the urge for advancement through self help, a concept universally believed in, which Samuel Smiles later summed up in his book on the subject published in 1859.

The trend towards the satisfaction of an increasing desire for knowledge and the prospects for improving one's situation in life, which vast numbers of new jobs created by the Industrial Revolution held out to many, received a special impetus in the Great Exhibition of 1851. This huge project, intended to impress foreign countries that promised a market for the industrial products of Britain, was also expected to serve as an inspiration to the workers of Britain and thus spur them to greater efforts. For Thomas Cook, the Exhibition provided an opportunity to expand his excursion business and, at the same time, to satisfy his own inherent idealism. The Great Exhibition was to be a Temperance affair, with only mineral waters available within its gates, which naturally pleased Cook, but it also would offer people an opportunity to educate themselves and therefore a justification for travelling to it.

Cook's involvement in the Great Exhibition came about through one of those chance meetings that so often change the course of a man's destiny. In 1850, Thomas Cook had decided to try his luck in America and was on his way to Liverpool to discuss with the shipping companies the terms under which he could take his passengers to the New World. On the way, he stopped at Derby and there met William Ellis and Joseph Paxton, both of whom were closely involved with the Midland Railway and with Temperance and, most important of all, with the Great Exhibition. They knew about Thomas Cook's early success in organizing excursion parties, and they now persuaded him to give up the idea of going to America and to undertake and promote excursions to the Great Exhibition in London instead.

Fired with enthusiasm for this new idea, and secure in the support of the Midland Railway, Cook set about making plans. First, he launched a new publication from his printing presses: *The Excursionist and Exhibition Advertiser*, perhaps the first travel newspaper, which Cook personally distributed through his

Having decided to venture all on a London office, Thomas Cook first tested the market by running a boarding house in Great Russell Street from which he operated his travel business. This invoice is for a three-day stay for £1.4s.0d.

friends in Temperance Societies and at street corners and factory gates. In the pages of this publication he set about persuading the public that they ought to travel, by publishing leading articles asking such questions as 'Why should the working man not go to the Great Exhibition?' These were aimed both at those working people who had doubts about their right to enjoy leisure and at their masters, who had to be persuaded it was their duty, and in their interest, to allow workers to visit the Exhibition. Cook followed up his leaders with others pointing out the educational value of the Great Exhibition.

'The particular advantage to be derived from visiting the Exhibition by all those employed in preparing and manufacturing cotton goods will be that Bolton, Manchester, Glasgow, Carlisle and Dundalk each and all will be (there) in friendly

Cook's Tours N.Y.

Ludgate Circus became the headquarters of Cook's business. He moved from Leicester to 98 Fleet Street in 1865 and soon after took over the whole corner building. This photo shows Cook's at a later date during a royal occasion involving King George V and Queen Mary.

competition in workmanship, raw material and variety of patterns, and will also be found in rivalship with the foreign producer of such goods,' he wrote. Such exhortations to the cotton industry were repeated for carpet makers, the iron trade, agricultural workers and many others.

His arguments, echoed in modern times by agents who deal in business travel, continually emphasize the need for business people to discover what their competitors are up to by personal visits, and seem very sophisticated for the period, revealing a natural flair for public relations which Cook showed over and over again.

As well as passengers, Cook needed the support of many railway companies so that he could combine his tour tickets over various lines at prices that would be attractive to passengers and leave him a profit. Thus he addressed himself to the railway proprietors:

If ever there was a time when the great power and astonishing facilities of the Railways should be most fully exerted on behalf of the population generally, surely 1851 is that time; and without recklessly jeopardizing the property of shareholders, every right-minded Director and Manager will feel that the utmost possible inducement should be held out for the millions to travel to London.

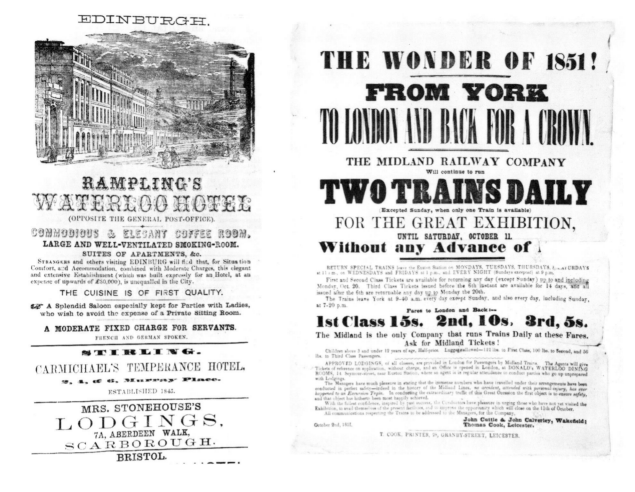

RAMPLING'S
WATERLOO HOTEL
(OPPOSITE THE GENERAL POST-OFFICE.)

COMMODIOUS & ELEGANT COFFEE ROOM.
LARGE AND WELL-VENTILATED SMOKING-ROOM.
SUITES OF APARTMENTS, &c.

Strangers and others visiting EDINBURG will find that, for Situation Comfort, and Accommodation, combined with Moderate Charges, this elegant and extensive Establishment (which was built expressly for an Hotel, at an expense of upwards of £30,000), is unequalled in the City.

THE CUISINE IS OF FIRST QUALITY.

☞ A Splendid Saloon especially kept for Parties with Ladies, who wish to avoid the expense of a Private Sitting Room.

A MODERATE FIXED CHARGE FOR SERVANTS.
FRENCH AND GERMAN SPOKEN.

STIRLING.
CARMICHAEL'S TEMPERANCE HOTEL,
2, 4, & 6, Murray Place.
ESTABLISHED 1843.

MRS. STONEHOUSE'S
LODGINGS,
7A, ABERDEEN WALK,
SCARBOROUGH.
BRISTOL.

THE WONDER OF 1851!
FROM YORK
TO LONDON AND BACK FOR A CROWN.
THE MIDLAND RAILWAY COMPANY
Will continue to run
TWO TRAINS DAILY
(Excepted Sunday, when only one Train is available)
FOR THE GREAT EXHIBITION,
UNTIL SATURDAY, OCTOBER 11.
Without any Advance of

RETURN SPECIAL TRAINS leave the Euston Station on MONDAYS, TUESDAYS, THURSDAYS, & SATURDAYS at 11 a.m., on WEDNESDAYS and FRIDAYS at 1 p.m., and EVERY NIGHT (Sundays excepted) at 9 p.m.

First and Second Class Tickets are available for returning any day (except Sunday) up to and including Monday, Oct. 20. Third Class Tickets issued before the 6th instant are available for 14 days, and all issued after the 6th are returnable any day up to Monday the 20th.

The Trains leave York at 9-40 a.m. every day except Sunday, and also every day, including Sunday, at 7-20 p.m.

Fares to London and Back :—
1st Class 15s. 2nd, 10s. 3rd, 5s.
The Midland is the only Company that runs Trains Daily at these Fares.
Ask for Midland Tickets !

Children above 3 and under 12 years of age, Half-price. Luggage allowed—112 lbs. in First Class, 100 lbs. in Second, and 56 lbs. to Third Class Passengers.

APPROVED LODGINGS, of all classes, are provided in London for Passengers by Midland Trains. The Agents will give Tickets of reference on application, without charge, and an Office is opened in London, at DONALD'S WATERLOO DINING ROOMS, 14 Seymour-street, near Euston Station, where an agent is in regular attendance to conduct parties who go up unprepared with Lodgings.

The Managers have much pleasure in stating that the immense numbers who have travelled under their arrangements have been conducted in perfect safety—indeed in the history of the Midland Lines, no accident, attended with personal injury, has ever happened to an Excursion Train. In conducting the extraordinary traffic of this Great Occasion the first object is to ensure safety, and that object has hitherto been most happily achieved.

With the fullest confidence, inspired by past success, the Conductors have pleasure in urging those who have not yet visited the Exhibition, to avail themselves of the present facilities, and to improve the opportunity which will close on the 11th of October.

All communications respecting the Trains to be addressed to the Managers, for the Company,

John Cattle & John Calverley, Wakefield;
Thomas Cook, Leicester.

October 2nd, 1851.

T. COOK, PRINTER, 28, GRANBY-STREET, LEICESTER.

While exhorting the public to travel to London, Cook also set about visiting the temperance societies, working men's clubs, and factories from which he hoped to draw many of his passengers. At the same time, he made arrangements in London for accommodation suitable for the parties of working people he intended to transport. One such arrangement was with the Ranelagh Club, a large establishment which he called the Mechanics Home for 1851. The Ranelagh Club was simply a vast lodging house that could cope with a thousand guests a night: Cook intended charging one shilling a night for bed and breakfast. Included in this price was a bedstead, good hair mattress, blankets, coverlid [bedcover], soap, towels, every convenience for ablution; boots and shoes were cleaned for an additional penny a pair.

By contemporary standards the price was reasonable though not cheap, considering that the average worker probably earned only a pound a week. As well as this the worker also had to pay his fare to London, which Cook fixed at fifteen shillings return.

Everything was set for a successful season when the rivalry of the newly established Great Northern Line knocked all Cook's and the Midland Railway's plans for six. To break into the market, the Great Northern was offering a discounted fare of five shillings. The battle was on.

ABOVE
Thomas Cook and his son, John Mason, took some 140,000 people to the Great Exhibition of 1851. Though he made no money out of it, the Exhibition traffic put Cook on the map throughout Britain.

TOP LEFT
In the 1860s Cook began to take advertisements in his *Excursionist* newspaper. Most of the hotels advertised were temperance ones. This one had a special saloon for ladies who could not afford a private sitting room (1863).

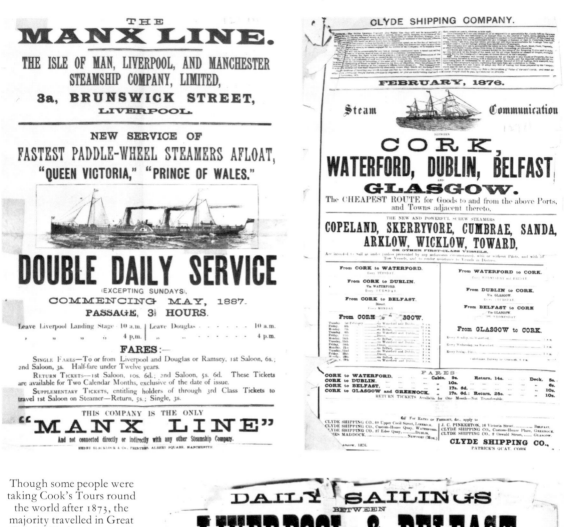

Though some people were taking Cook's Tours round the world after 1873, the majority travelled in Great Britain. Cook represented practically all available forms of transport and sold tickets for such local services as the Manx Line, throughout the century.

With a quick change of strategy, Cook offered to come to a new arrangement with the Midland Railway. If they agreed to a new low fare to meet the competition he would guarantee to provide more passengers to compensate for the lower profits. It was a situation which was to be repeated often in the evolution of the business of travel and one which has more than once hit the headlines in modern times.

Cook immediately set to work, calling for support from his wife Marianne and his son John Mason, now sixteen. His visits to prospective excursionists increased; he took entire trains to the very doors of factories, along their freight lines, and there he would greet the workers with a brass band and exhortations to join the excursions to the Great Exhibition. As soon as a train was filled, it would set off for London accompanied either by Cook or by his son; both worked night and day for two months ferrying the parties to and fro.

To accommodate those who did not have the ready cash, Cook set himself up as an amateur pawnbroker, accepting watches, gold chains and other objects of value as collateral for the tickets.

Writing to royalty was a ploy he was often to use as a public relations exercise— one which earned him the applause and loyalty of his customers. In 1851, he found time to write to Prince Albert to request that in the interests of visitors from the regions the one shilling Exhibition ticket should be valid for four days instead of one. At the same time, he wrote to the newspapers complaining that metropolitan fares had gone up by thirty per cent since the beginning of the Exhibition, and that a 'vile crew of harpies and sharpers were ever waiting to pounce on the unsuspecting'.

In reply to a criticism that his parties were noisy and rude and that there was a great deal of drunkenness among the passengers, he was quick to turn the accusation to his advantage, denying that this was a general evil and saying that the spectacle of a drunk man was odious rather than agreeable to fellow passengers and therefore it had the effect of putting others off drink. He followed this by quoting what he claimed to be an actual example of a passenger who had been tempted by drink but saved as a result of an encounter with an inebriated one.

It would be easy to accuse Cook of opportunism, and of looking the other way when his principles threatened his profits, but this would be unfair. Although an idealist and philanthropist, he was a practical man who saw the world in a broader perspective than does a zealot. He wanted to change it but within the terms of what was possible, an attitude that helped him to build up his travel business without those head-on confrontations that sometimes spell disaster in enterprises.

Even before the Great Exhibition, Cook had realized that apart from the price of tickets, one of the deterrents to popular travel was the difficulty of obtaining 'through' tickets. In a nation in which thousands of railway companies operated separate sections of most lines, it was necessary to obtain several tickets to travel any distance at all.

Thomas Cook created two systems to make the acquisition of tickets and use of different routes easier. One was his excursions system by which he would charter a train or carriages and conduct the whole party himself (a system which later came popularly to be called the Cook's Tour), and the other was his tourist ticket system, which he named the Circular Ticket. The tourist ticket system was one by which the traveller would purchase tickets for specific routes devised by Thomas Cook, then set off on his own from his destination and use the tickets as required, or change them for other tickets should he want to alter his route. Unused tickets could be returned to Cook for a refund at the end of the journey.

One of the first holiday brochures to the Continent to have a coloured cover (*c.* 1900).

All the shipping lines sailing out of
Britain to all parts of the world were
included in this series of sailing lists
(*c.* 1890).

LEFT
Every tourist who could afford one carried a telescope, as did the men who went to the seaside to watch the ladies bathing.

RIGHT
Though tourists to the Channel resorts of France increased rapidly, few of them wanted to establish contact with the natives (as this *Punch* cartoon suggests).

BELOW
At Ramsgate, one of the many hundreds of seaside resorts made accessible by the railways, the train deposited excursionists right on the beach.

AT A FRENCH WATERING-PLACE.

Mother. "TOMMY, WHY DON'T YOU TRY TO TALK TO THOSE OTHER CHILDREN IN THEIR OWN LANGUAGE?"
Youthful Briton. "WHAT'S THE GOOD? IT ONLY ENCOURAGES THEM!"

Ramsgate Sands.

Although this system must have meant an enormous amount of work for Cook, both in negotiating the terms of his commission and in accounting for the vast range of tickets over the scores of railway lines that he selected for his tours, it must also have been beneficial in that he was paid in advance for tickets which might never be used and therefore his cash position was assured.

On his successful North Wales and Scottish operations, Thomas Cook used both systems and it was a bitter blow to him when the Scottish railways took away his excursion concession in 1862, the Scottish railways having decided to run the excursion business themselves, thus saving agency commission. There may have been more to the decision than that. Excursion trains were quoted at a lower fare than the Tourist ticket because they were, in fact, a charter arrangement by which Thomas Cook took on the total responsibility for the train and ran it as a conducted excursion. Since his profit margins were minimal, Cook usually conducted the excursions himself or pressed his young son and even his wife into service as travelling courier. It could be that on some occasions there was no-one to accompany the train. Certainly the Scottish railways appear to have accused Cook of using the excursion train benefit to undercut their own fares while not complying with the obligation to provide a courier. Cook said that there was sometimes an overlap between two kinds of traffic and added that the deprivation of his excursion concession would mean that Scotland would lose some 6,000 visitors as he no longer had 'any inducement to accompany Highland parties because no parties can be convened to call for our assistance or company'.

Though the end of the Scottish excursion business was a blow, it did not stop the steady progress of Cook's business. He was busy extending his excursion and tourist

The arrival of a Cook's party in Paris at the Gare du Nord was recorded by an *Illustrated London News* artist as early as 1861.

The Flying Man poster was
first used at the turn of the
century and later re-used with
contemporary passengers on
the genii's back.

OPPOSITE
Passengers on Nile steamers
each received a printed
passenger-list with an
attractive cover (*c.* 1890).

As a tourist destination,
Ireland was popular for its
sport and romantic history
(*c.* 1890).

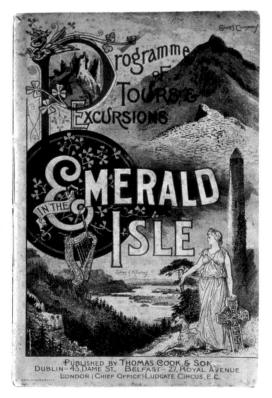

Ostend was an important
Channel port for tourists
going to Belgium and
Germany, and it also offered
resort facilities including a
magnificent Kursaal.

systems to other parts of Britain, including visits to every town and city where there
was an exhibition, such as Dublin in 1853 and Manchester in 1856.

He always found time for the cause of temperance, to provide help for the needy,
whether they were poor fishermen on Iona or starving workers in Leicester (to
whom he once sent bargeloads of potatoes). He also had the time and energy to
express himself on other matters such as the celebration of the anniversary of the
Battle of Waterloo, which he regarded as a waste of time and a misguided celebration
of war when everyone should have been thinking about the encouragement of peace
and the idea of a great teetotal demonstration by all nations.

The Scottish blow of 1862 was softened by the opportunity to repeat his
successes of 1851 at the International Exhibition of 1862 in London. This time,
however, Midland Railways decided to look after the rail traffic themselves.
Dismayed but not defeated, Cook decided to concentrate his energies on the hotel
business. Learning that a tenement block was being built in London's Fulham Road
opposite Pelham Crescent, Cook made a bid for it and began immediately to
advertise the tenements in *The Excursionist*. The rooms, two hundred in number,
were suitable for groups made up of relations, friends or parties of from two to six
persons and, being new, were 'free of bugs'.

The chocolate manufacturing firm of Fry and Sons; Allbright and Wilson's
chemical works; the Huddersfield works of John Brooks, and W. E. Forster's
factory from Bradford all sent parties to Cook's tenement building. There were also
parties of workers from Germany and Italy.

Once more, Cook had a success on his hands and he was even obliged to look for
more buildings to house the overflow.

In the midst of all this activity, Cook had also found yet another field of
enterprise which offered infinite opportunities: the seaside.

Trips to the sea had begun to become popular in the eighteenth century when
some notable quacks like Dr Richard Russell set about exploiting the interest in their
health of the classes of people who frequented mineral spas. Dr Russell's proposition
was that sea water was just as health-giving as mineral water and he promoted the

Tourists landed at St Malo for their tour to Dinard, which grew into a major holiday resort for British people.

idea of bathing in it and even drinking it, though he advised mixing it with milk or port to make it more appetising.

Russell's ideas provided a justification for seaside holidays, but the means of getting there for the general public was provided by steam-powered transport, first off all the waterways that linked great cities like London and Manchester to the sea and later by the railways.

Where the railways went there went Cook and by the 1850s he was busy providing his circular tickets to the newly developing resorts, as well as to the well-established seaside watering places such as Scarborough, which rejoiced in the possession of a fresh-water spring as well as infinite quantities of North Sea water.

One of the problems at a time when trains were slow and journeys were further delayed by derailments, line subsidence, obstructions by cattle and other hazards was how to offer day trips to the sea which gave a reasonable number of hours by the briny. Cook solved this by starting his chartered trains at midnight. His main business was one which was gaining him more and more customers: the circular ticket covering direct journeys over a variety of railway lines.

Having established his ticket system to the Yorkshire and Lancashire coasts he now made arrangements for trips to the West Country, a region that was then almost unknown to people from the cities of Britain because of its distance and lack of communications. Having had no success at persuading the South Wales Railway to give him a fare concession to Bristol, he made an arrangement with the Great Western and arranged a tour by stage coach and train which included the north coasts of Devon and Cornwall and a stay at Torquay, which, Cook pointed out, was patronized by Her Imperial Highness the Grand Duchess Marie of Russia.

In the south Cook came to an arrangement with the Brighton and South Coast Railway which opened up to him business opportunities in Brighton, Hastings, Eastbourne, Havant, Hayling, Littlehampton, Newhaven, Shoreham, Southsea, St Leonards, Worthing and the Isle of Wight. But by now Cook was looking farther afield and while keeping his British traffic growing he launched himself into the Continent.

CHAPTER THREE

In the Steps of Milord

Big fleas have little fleas on their backs to bite them and little fleas have smaller fleas and so on *ad infinitum*, and what is true for fleas is also true for excursionists, tourists and travellers. As the working-class crowds began to invade the seaside resorts of Britain their traditional visitors began to look for other places to which they could escape. Inevitably, their eyes fell upon the European resorts patronized by the aristocratic and wealthy, who in their turn looked for more select resorts away from the new Continental tourists.

But the search for new resorts in Europe did not lead Cook's tourists to the sea, for they were not yet the hedonists of later years but earnest people seeking a cultural upgrading, and therefore they visited those towns and cities which had marked the peregrinations of that class of person whose education was not complete until he had done the Grand Tour of Europe. By visiting these places, the tourists felt that something of the gloss of their social superiors descended on their shoulders and, as many of them were the teachers, doctors and clergy who served the upper classes, they reasonably hoped that in the course of time the closing of the cultural gap would lead to the bridging of the social gap as well.

Long-term British residents of such places as Florence, Venice, Nice and Interlaken did not take kindly to the arrival of their worthy and ambitious inferiors. They had no desire to encourage the thirst for information of those who arrived, Baedeker in hand, behind the coat tails of Thomas Cook.

For Cook himself, professional people, whose status hovered between that of tradesman and the leisured class, were a new and exciting market to serve, and in the 1850s he began to woo them and their employers as a few years earlier he had wooed the British workers.

'Deacons and wealthy members of churches and congregations,' he appealed. 'Do what is necessary to liberate your pastors from study and the unceasing public and onerous labour; provide them, if they are in circumstances not to provide for themselves, with the means of a trip and you will have a reward in their lengthened lives and pulpit and pastoral efficiency.'

While campaigning to find passengers, he still had to continue negotiations with railway companies in Britain and Europe. At first the Brighton and South Coast Railway would not work with him, so his first tour to the Paris Exhibition in 1855 had to take a circuitous route via Harwich, Antwerp, Brussels and Cologne, down the Rhine to Strasbourg and so to Paris. Cook made the best of this arrangement and his efforts were rewarded by the first of many reports written by his clients. This one was penned by a lady who signed herself 'Matilda and her sisters'. Matilda was in raptures at Mr Cook's arrangements and fulsome in her praise.

'We found the greatest comfort in having such a friend as Mr Cook to whom to look in every difficulty, to take from us the perplexity of selecting hotels, arranging

The first big thrill of a Continental tour was the Channel crossing. Here passengers are boarding the steamer at Dieppe on their return to England (*c.* 1920).

The early tourists (*c.* 1900) crossed the Channel on paddle steamers but later they were conveyed on screw-driven ships of a type similar to some still in service today.

with landlords, procuring railway tickets, exchanging money or learning the times of trains.'

Ladies were to be the mainstay of Cook parties throughout the century and he looked after them assiduously, praising them for their perspicacity in travelling on his tours and assuring them that they would be quite safe in his hands and never lonely. 'Even those who start out alone,' he told them, 'will often find an agreeable companion.'

The total cost of the Paris trip was £10 and the good value that a Cook holiday offered was not overlooked by his passengers, who proclaimed his excellence far and wide.

Though it was to be almost another twenty years before Thomas Cook launched his traveller's cheque system, it is interesting to note that at this time he was already

The pier, designed to provide a landing stage on tidal coasts, became a popular place for promenading. Excursionists to Ostend must have been pleased to find this familiar feature of an English resort on a foreign strand (*c.* 1900).

A German artist's view of British tourists heading for Paris (*c.* 1860).

Les Anglais vus par les Français

Engländer auf der Reise nach Paris

Zeichnungen von Gustave Doré (1861)

Engländer stürmen auf den Zug, der sie nach Paris bringt.

involved with foreign exchange transactions for his clients. Soon after the Paris trip, having made arrangements for tourist tickets with the Paris, Lyons, Mediterranean Railway, he announced that he could also handle foreign exchange transactions.

In 1863 came one of the great moments of his career. Having at last succeeded in coming to terms with the Brighton and South Coast railways and having his route through France ensured by the Paris, Lyons Mediterranean Railway he announced a trip to Switzerland and Mont Blanc.

It is hard today to conceive of the glamour of such an expedition. In 1863, the Alps were the wonder of the world and the conquerors of their peaks, the British, were heroes. Moreover, Byron, Shelley and other writers of the Romantic Movement had created a scene in which mountains, cliffs, chasms, gorges and torrents were all charged with emotional meaning.

Over five hundred people replied to Cook's first advertisement, which appeared in 1863. Most of them decided to accompany him only as far as Paris, but one hundred and twenty went with him all the way to Mont Blanc.

Among the latter was a Miss Jemima Morrell who, with her brother, was one of a group of young people who travelled with this first party to Switzerland with Thomas Cook. Like many travellers of the period, Miss Morrell kept a journal in

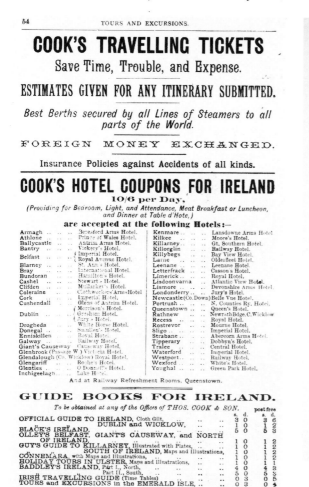

"KIT BAG ESCAPE."

The colonization of Africa which took part from the last decade of the nineteenth century made the topographical features described by explorers and settlers into tourist pilgrimage spots. The Victoria Falls were particularly popular.

One of the many brochures offering Cook's Tours to Egypt (*c.* 1904).

OPPOSITE
This Cook's Tour brochure of the turn of the century was sold to the public through W. H. Smith bookstands.

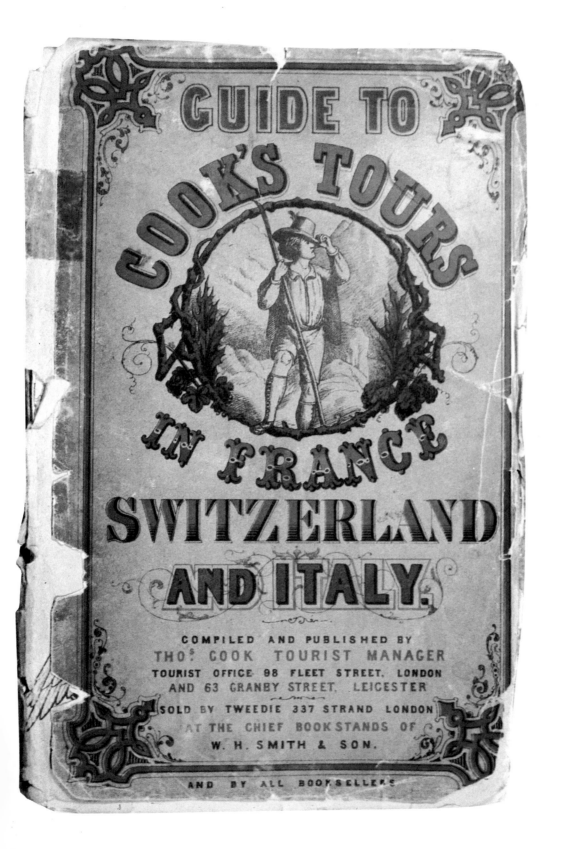

GUIDE TO
COOK'S TOURS
IN FRANCE
SWITZERLAND
AND ITALY.

COMPILED AND PUBLISHED BY
THO.⁵ COOK TOURIST MANAGER
TOURIST OFFICE 98 FLEET STREET, LONDON
AND 63 GRANBY STREET, LEICESTER
SOLD BY TWEEDIE 337 STRAND LONDON
AT THE CHIEF BOOKSTANDS OF
W. H. SMITH & SON.

AND BY ALL BOOKSELLERS.

RIGHT
Among the hazards of foreign travel were bed bugs and other undesirable insects. Doyle, the famous Victorian cartoonist, depicted the midnight bug hunt.

THE RIGHT OF SEARCH

BELOW
Meals at hotels were usually eaten at large tables. In the background Doyle shows the musical entertainment provided, and one of the musicians (left) makes the collection.

BELOW
Gambling was a popular form of entertainment at German spas from where it moved to Monte Carlo and the Mediterranean resorts.

which she recorded the details of the journey through Geneva, Montreux, Leukerbad, Kandersteg, Interlaken, Lucerne, the Rigi mountain and Neuchatel. In her neat calligraphy and with illustrations and decorations to enliven the pages, Miss Morrell wrote an account of her group, which she named the Junior Alpine Club, and left a vivid picture of the people and the places that were to become the highspots of a Thomas Cook tour for over a century.

The journal, which is now in the Thomas Cook archives, along with other diaries and ephemera of travel, ends with the words 'Account of a tour in Switzerland and France—June 26 to July 16, 1863, twenty one days inclusive £19.17s.6d.'

Cook followed up his first Swiss success with another tour the same year, using both of them to build up his own contacts with hotel keepers, guides and railway officials on the journey. As a result of his experience he was able to give an exact description of the itinerary to his future travellers.

Departure from London Bridge or Victoria was at 6 am and Newhaven was reached at 8.45 am. After crossing the Channel, which might be a lengthy business if the tide was unsuitable or the sea rough, passengers disembarked at Dieppe, at about 2 or 3 pm and were given a hot dinner. This was supplied by Monsieur Jules who regaled his British guests with soup, fish, joints of beef or mutton, potatoes, peas, cheese and salad, all for two francs.

Passports were not required but Cook recommended that they should be carried, one passport being sufficient for a whole party and though men had to be named it was only necessary to give the number of women in the party.

Arrival in Paris was scheduled for 8 pm and the party stayed the night at the London and New York Hotel which cost 6s.6d. For those who stayed in Paris, Cook arranged excursions by train to Versailles and Fontainebleau, having negotiated a concessionary fare. He also organized *voitures* for a ride round the Bois de Boulogne for his transit passengers, offering a subtle inducement for taking the ride by mentioning in his description that, while in the Bois, one of his parties had passed by the Empress Eugenie and the Prince Imperial riding in their own coach.

In this description of the itinerary, Cook remarks on his pleasure at seeing numerous British working men who appear to be enjoying themselves and to whom he offered the reduced price railway fare that he had arranged for a trip to Versailles.

From Paris, the Swiss excursionists took the Paris, Lyons, Mediterranean Railway, about which Cook complained because it travelled at only 25 miles per hour, arriving at Geneva at 11 pm. The distance, says Cook, is 388 miles and he points out that those who find this too long a journey can stop overnight at Lyons, Dijon or Macon on his tourist ticket.

The fare for this tour from London was £6 return, first class, and included a guide, whom, Cook says ingenuously, was to have been an intelligent German, who, since he did not show up, was replaced by a Swiss teacher.

The price was reduced for children, though Cook made it quite clear that he did not want any on his tours.

'We hope,' he wrote in his tour description, 'that the infantile race will stop in their nurses' arms and that the next grade above them, under seven, will not be taken to Switzerland.'

After the success of his first Swiss trips, Cook during the following winter crossed the Alps by sledge and diligence [stage-coach] drawn by thirteen mules, as there were no railways, and set about arranging tours to Italy.

Switzerland was the first popular holiday country. Most of the journeys within its boundaries were by diligence. This one is about to go over the Simplon Pass (1890).

The Rigi mountain above the Lac des Quatre Cantons (rechristened Lake Lucerne by the English tourists), was a favourite pilgrimage spot for sun worshippers.

His reconnoitring took him to Turin, where he took the railway to Milan, Piacenza, Parma, Modena, and Bologna, then over the Appenines by diligence to Pistoia where he picked up the railway again to Florence. From Florence he went to Leghorn where he had a set-to with the touts who hung around every port and railway station hoping to pick up guests for those hotels which had agreed to give the commissions. His encounter, he said, convinced him of everything that was written in guide books about hotel touts whose rudeness and greediness were every bit as bad as they were described.

What the Italians thought of this busy, bald-headed little figure in his practical serge suit who spoke no word of Italian, is not recorded.

Despite his lack of language, by the end of his tour Cook had convinced railway companies and hoteliers of the efficacy of his ticket and coupon system and was then ready to set up a series of Italian Tours which quickly became the most sought-after of all his arrangements.

Everyone stopped at Paris on the way to Switzerland and for many it was their main holiday destination. Walking in the Champs Elysees was a must, and the daring ones rode on the wooden horses of the merry-go-rounds, seen here on the left and right of this drawing from *The Illustrated London News*.

Among the entertainments provided in Switzerland, boating ranked high. It was more romantic than climbing mountains and less trouble. This party are on the Vierwald Stattersee— otherwise Lake Lucerne (1851).

Italy was a perfect territory for Cook's Tours. It satisfied the tourists' desire to follow in the steps of their social superiors, it justified, because of its history, the taking of a holiday there (for, after all, were not the British the Romans of the present day?), it spread warm feelings of benevolence in all the travellers, who threw coins for street urchins to fight over or who bestowed their patronage on selected boatmen, mule drivers and other servants of the open-handed British traveller.

Moreover, and remembering that Cook's parties consisted in the main of women, Italy was a land that reflected the romanticism of contemporary culture. The Italians, with their dark good looks and flashing eyes, were the epitome of all the heroes of classical Greece and Rome and their courtesy and gallantry aroused unspeakable thoughts in ladies' minds.

As far as the British male traveller was concerned, he felt a certain superiority at the comparison between Britain's success and Italy's lack of it, and accepted with patronizing complacency the title of 'milord' which Italian servants bestowed on

ABOVE
The Hotel Jungfrau at Wengen with its fine view of the mountains was popular with English visitors (*c.* 1880)

LEFT
Tours to Switzerland were justified by many on the grounds that they were good for the health. Swiss spas flourished and at Loeche-les-Bains, or Leukerbad, mixed bathing, in voluminous garments, was allowed. Bathers were served breakfast on floating trays and some even managed to read the papers while immersed.

BELOW
The Hotel des Alpes at Montreux on Lake Geneva was typical of the new hotels built to accommodate the Cook's Tourists. The railway which brought them can be seen running alongside the lake (*c.* 1861).

him. Meanwhile, the Italians smiled and genuflected and kept their real but good-humoured thoughts to themselves, as history had taught them to do.

Sunshine was not one of the attractions of Italy as it is today, but culture was and Cook soon developed a subsidiary line of business selling guide books by Baedeker, Murray, Chambers and his competitor in the tourist field, Henry Gaze. In 1874 he entered the guide book business in earnest, associating himself with Simpkin Marshall of New York to produce a series of comprehensive guide books which the company continued to publish until 1939.

The cultural aspirations of the Cookites, as they came to be called, did not impress the seasonal British residents who lived in palatial villas or in the suites of rooms designed to provide private accommodation for whole families in the Grand Hotels. These expatriates, who followed a tradition that can be traced back to

From Switzerland, the land of romantic scenery, the tourists went on to Italy, where they rhapsodised over its romantic history. At first there were no railways and spring crossings were made by sledge (1873).

In summer the Alpine roads could be negotiated by post coaches, which as this painting shows carried an armed guard (1873).

A winter sports brochure published about
1920 and designed to persuade the ladies to
take Cook's winter sports holidays.

OPPOSITE
The emancipated woman of the 1920s took to
winter sports, perhaps because this kind of
holiday provided the thrills and freedom that
symbolised their new position in society.

WINTER SPORT
THOS COOK & SONS
ARRANGEMENTS

R.A.Shuffrey
1910

In 1869 the Mont Cenis Railway tunnel opened a new route to Italy which was described by the Empire-conscious *Illustrated London News* as 'the route to India' as it shortened the distance to the East by connecting London to Brindisi by rail.

Renaissance times when nobility knew no frontiers, resented the intrusion of tourists of an inferior station to their own in what until now they had regarded as their privileged domains.

Their feelings about the Cook's tourists were expressed by James Lever, the British Consul at La Spezia, who wrote under the pen name of Cornelius O'Dowd.

'These devil's dust tourists,' O'Dowd complained, 'have spread over Europe injuring our credit and damaging our character. Their gross ignorance is the very smallest of their sins. It is their overbearing insolence, their purse strong insistence, their absurd pretentions to be in a place abroad that they have never dreamed of aspiring at home—all these claims suggesting to the foreigner that he is in the presence of a very distinguished and exalted representative of Great Britain'.

O'Dowd's outburst provided Cook with the opportunity he relished and he tore into him in defence of his customers, winning their admiration and support as the champion of their right to privileges formerly enjoyed only by the few.

Attacks on the Cookites came only from their compatriots, for the Swiss and the Italians were overjoyed at the prospects that were opening before them. An enormous activity began in the building of railways and hotels in the countries visited by British tourists.

One of the pioneers among the hoteliers was Peter Ober, an Alsatian who was tutor to an English family at Interlaken. Here, with the help of his employers, he

48

bought a house which he ran first as a boarding house and later as the Hotel Ober. Another was Friedrich Seiler, a Swiss who had interest in a wood business in Unterseen and in the Bodeli and Brunig Railways. He later built the Grand Hotel Jungfrau at Interlaken and his pupil Edward Ruchti created the Grand Hotel Victoria, also on the Hoheweg in the same resort. Another Interlaken hotelier was a Johan Strubin, who built the Schweizerhof. Three brothers Knechternhofer developed the steamer services on Lakes Thun and Brienz.

It is not surprising that Interlaken was the centre of the fast-growing hotel industry in Switzerland, for it was the centre for the Bernese Oberland which was the Mecca for British tourists and one of the main destinations for those who travelled with Thomas Cook. Another favourite tourist area was Lucerne and here Maximillian Von Pfyffer Altishofen built the Hotel National, an Italian palace-style building in which the young Cesar Ritz began his great career.

The names of the great hoteliers proliferated in Switzerland. There was the Badrutt family, the first to encourage winter visitors, and the installers of the Cresta run with the encouragement of British guests; the Baurs, whose name is commemorated at the famous Hotel Baur au Lac in Zurich; and the Fassbinds who

The crossing of the Alps made cheap tours possible and Cook began a series of such tours in 1864. The size of the Colosseum in Rome and the horrors of its history caught the public imagination (*c.* 1880).

1908.

PICTURESQUE DOVEDALE

Holiday
TOURS

Organised by
THOS. COOK & SON

LOVELY LUCERNE

An early Continental holiday brochure;
the interior pages were all in
monochrome (*c.* 1908).

In 1911 the Cooks produced this map of the Trossachs for their tourists.

were connected with the Rigi hotels and the Vitznau-Rigi railway which took and still takes thousands of tourists to the sunrise-watching ritual at the top of the mountain.

All the great hotels, many of which still stand in their rococo splendour, were used by Cook for his middle-class clientele, which, as the century progressed, greatly increased in numbers.

In more recent times the glories of the great Swiss hotels have been enjoyed by a more democratic cross-section of society travelling on package holidays, for in just over one hundred years the Cookites have stepped into the milords' shoes and thus fulfilled the dreams of the man who put travel abroad within their reach.

Florence was the city of the Medicis, a banking family that Victorian business people could understand. Many of them devoted large sums to finishing off the buildings that the Florentines had left unfinished. This drawing from an 1870s book on Italy shows the Ducal Palace and the Uffizi, or offices, now an art gallery.

CHAPTER FOUR

The American Connection

In 1865 the headquarters of the Cook's Tours system moved from Leicester to London, where Cook staked all he possessed on a building at 98 Fleet Street. The ground floor was set up as an office for the public, and here Cook sold every ancillary to travel he could think of in order to make the necessary profit to cover his overheads and interest payments. His shelves displayed guide books, travelling baggage (including a Gladstone bag which could be converted into a fire escape by virtue of a rope and pulley), telescopes, footwear, and water purifiers. He also ran an advertisement agency for London and provincial newspapers.

On the upper floors his wife started a Temperance Hotel along the lines of the one in Leicester. These were also the family living quarters.

Desperate for help but unable to afford outsiders, Cook called in all his family to lend a hand, including his son who was working as a printer in Leicester. John Mason demurred at working with his father and wrote to say that it would never work out as they had been unable to agree on business matters in the past. Cook insisted and so, no doubt, did his wife and John Mason became manager of the London office.

The Fleet Street headquarters was an immediate success as Londoners flocked to avail themselves of the benefits of the Cook's Tour and Excursion systems. Not only

Thomas Cook arrived in the United States in 1865 and his first tour was led by his son John Mason in 1866. Although much impressed by the railways, he thought them slow. This drawing from Dickens' *Notes on America* shows the social life on a train. Cook was delighted to find the iced water dispensers seen here in the corner of the carriage (*c.* 1880).

Long distance travel in
America was more
comfortable than in Europe
as this dining car drawing
shows. Pullman's ideas
inspired Nagelmackers to
create a luxury train system in
Europe (c. 1880).

the public, but railway managers and hotel owners, even those who had thought that they could handle their own sales, arrived to visit Cook.

'We are now besieged,' says Thomas Cook in a note in *The Excursionist*, 'with applications from very respectable Hotel Proprietors to give the benefit of our recommendations to their establishements.'

In the sudden flush of success, Cook launched himself into projects that had been in his mind for years. First, he revived his plans to set up business with America and began to prepare for his first visit. He armed himself with recommendations including one from the Under Secretary to the Colonies, Edward Foster, and one from John Bright who praised him for his enterprise with the words, 'If you can assist some hundreds of Englishmen to visit the United States in the course of the year, and as many Americans to visit England, you will be of service to both countries.'

Before he set off Cook addressed the people of America through *The Excursionist*:

In England and Scotland more than a million tourists and excursionists have availed themselves of my arrangements; tens of thousands have travelled with me, making it a yearly practice to make a trip under my arrangements. These have been my best advertisers in as much as they have recommended my tours to their respective circles of friends and neighbours . . . My own Continental Tours have reached a point of interest and solidity which gives me encouragement to combine with them the interest of another Continent; and in America, too, there is now a field of operation of unparalleled scope and interest.

Cook sailed to America on the *City of Boston*, one of the Inman Line ships which had begun to combine comfort and speed in the Transatlantic crossings. After years of experiment and failure with such ships as the *Great Britain* and the *Great Eastern*, shipping companies had developed screw-driven, iron-hulled ships which were capable of taking passengers, many of whom were immigrants, safely, quickly, and reliably to America.

Once more, Cook was launching an extension to his Cook's Tour System at an opportune moment. When he arrived in America the Civil War had been over only a few months and the country was still in a state of turmoil. The coast-to-coast railway had not yet been completed but, undeterred, Cook toured to Montreal, Toronto, Hamilton, Niagara Falls, Detroit, Chicago, Springfield, Cincinnati, Philadelphia, Baltimore and Washington. By the time he returned to New York, he had covered ten thousand miles by steamer and rail and was more persuaded than ever that the new United States was ready for his excursion system.

During the course of his visit, Cook made arrangements with railway companies by which he obtained a concessionary fare of two-thirds of a penny a mile but, following his personal trip with an excursion conducted by his son, he found that his agreements were not being honoured.

'It is annoying that petty jealousies and unforeseen obstacles have prevented the free, full operations of our Transatlantic arrangements,' he wrote. Not only was his two-thirds of a penny fare not being given to his parties, but a further setback was that his own agents in Britain were accusing him of accepting accommodation inferior to that promised to his clients.

It was not an auspicious start, but John Mason Cook was made of even firmer

COOK'S ANGLO-AMERICAN AND EUROPEAN TOURS.

FIRST CABIN RETURN TICKETS,
Are now issued by Mr. Cook, at Reduced Fares, from

PARIS, LONDON, LIVERPOOL OR GLASGOW,
TO THE

UNITED STATES & CANADA.
AVAILABLE BY SIX LINES OF STEAMERS.

At Fares varying from 20 Guineas to 30 Guineas,

Allowing Passengers to return at any time within Six or Twelve Months; giving a choice of the following Steamers.

SAILINGS OF STEAMERS AND REGULATIONS FOR RETURNING.

SINGLE JOURNEY TICKETS

From Paris, London, Liverpool, or Glasgow, are issued by Mr. Cook, to any part of America.

EMIGRATION TICKETS.

COOK'S AMERICAN TRAVELLER'S GAZETTE

Excursionist & Tourist Advertiser.

EDITED AND PUBLISHED BY
THOS. COOK & SON
261 BROADWAY, NEW YORK

Established 1851
Vol. 54
Fifty-fourth Year

No. 1—January, 1904
Price Ten Cents
One Dollar per Annum

Originators of the European Tourist and Excursion System, Established 1841

GENERAL PASSENGER AGENTS IN AMERICA FOR THE MIDLAND RAILWAY OF ENGLAND

CONTENTS

---

stuff than his father. He renegotiated the entire deal with the American railway companies, issuing a series of forty-one tourist tickets, and tied up five shipping companies for his Transatlantic arrangements. The Cooks intended to develop traffic both to and from America and to include in their arrangements the mass transportation of emigrants who were now heading for the land of opportunity from Britain and Europe.

At the end of 1865, Cook announced the excursion which his son would lead to America in April of the following year. He offered a number of departure points for the same reason as modern tour operators do for their package holidays: to enlarge his catchment area. His passengers could sail to New York by the Inman Line from Liverpool or the Guion Line; from Glasgow by Handyside and Henderson; or to Quebec by the James and Alexander Allan Line. They could also sail by the Allan Brothers Line to Canada from Liverpool.

The Cook ticket, renegotiated by John Mason, entitled passengers to a two-thirds discount on rail travel in the United States, a special reduction because the railways had not yet got out of the trough created by the Civil War. In Canada the reduction was only one-third of the normal fare.

The Railways that were prepared to give Cook his reduced fares were the Hudson River Railroad, the Reusselaer and Saratoga, the Rutland and Burlington, the Vermont and Canada, the Erie, the New York Central, the Atalantic and Great Western, the Cincinnati, the Ohio and Mississipi, the Illinois Central and the

American business to Europe was so good that Cook launched his Circular Note in New York in 1872. Though he called this a traveller's 'check' in his description of it Cook used the word 'Circular' to identify the cheques with his Circular ticket system.

Michigan Central. In Canada he had the support of the Grand Trunk and Great Western of Canada.

Two features of the American railways which had pleased Cook enormously were the supply of iced water, and the provision of sleeping cars, which were virtually unknown in Europe at this time.

'It is a great convenience in travelling over these long American lines of railway to be able to take a berth and sleep away the hours that afford no prospect of country scenery or active life,' he had written after his first visit, and the fact that his train had gone off the rails, delaying his journey by twelve hours, did not change his opinion.

John Mason was equally impressed by everything he saw in America though, like his father, he complained about the lack of speed of American trains which averaged only fifteen to twenty miles an hour. On his first conducted tour he covered some 4,000 miles in the United States and including the Transatlantic journey, some ten thousand miles in all. It was a long and wearisome six weeks for him, especially as he was not only acting as courier but also making contacts with people he hoped to do business with, as well as old friends and acquaintances who had emigrated from Leicester. At the end of it John Mason wrote, 'I flatter myself that even our American friends must admit that nobody but a "Britisher" would have been able to successfully cope with such difficulties.' As became evident in the following years, he felt himself to be one of a race cast in a heroic mould and destined to lead the world towards a millenium.

Most of the transatlantic steamship lines kept going by carrying mail and emigrants. As late as 1906 Cunard were offering a fare of £3 under the Family Settlement Scheme.

A feature of the conducted tours to America was a tour of the Civil War battlefields. On his return from his first tour, John Mason Cook reported on his trip from Philadelphia to Baltimore on the Wilmington Line.

This short ride was one of great interest, as it brought us into contact with the first views we had of the scenes of the late war. We had to cross the Gunpowder and Bush rivers' contemporary bridges, one three quarters and one a mile in length, the original ones being destroyed in the engagements; we also had the novelty of having a whole train and engine ferried across the Susquehanna river, on one ferry boat. We arrived at Baltimore at 8.00 pm and stayed at the Maltby House, which is situated in one of the streets where an engagement took place. We stayed at Baltimore until 5.00 pm on Thursday when we left by the Steamboat *James T. Brady* of the New Line for Richmond; our route being one of

British shipping advertising was more traditional, though here the couple have the appearance of Hollywood celebrities.

In 1893 the Cooks took part in the Chicago Exhibition and promoted world travel among Chicagoans with this special brochure.

great interest through Chesapeake beyond the James River, passing many ever-to-be-remembered points of the great struggle, such as Norfolk, Fort Munroe, Harrisons Landing, Malvern Hill, Dutch Gap canal, Butler's Look Out etc etc.

Outside the city of Richmond at Fort Harrison the party came into more immediate contact with the battlefield.

The wooden huts that had been headquarters for officers were now used as pigsties, poultry houses and goat houses, for the negroes and other workmen and their families employed in making a cemetery for the bones of the killed. Seventy men were employed for that purpose at the time of our visit. We were conducted to a spinney about one mile to the right of the principal earthworks, where the ground was lost and regained several times in a few hours and in that part we saw skulls, arms, legs etc bleaching in the sun. In some parts we saw large heaps of bones, some of horses, and the bones of animals slaughtered as food for the armies.

In 1871 Cook took an American partner. He was a man called Jenkins who had been a member of a special party of Knights Templars for whom Thomas Cook had arranged a tour to Europe. A company called Cook, Son and Jenkins was formed and an office opened at 362 Broadway, New York in 1873. Jenkins was an enthusiast with the large, optimistic vision of his nation. He believed that Cook could become the leader in the American tourist business just as he was in Europe.

Though hopeful, the Cooks were more cautious. They soon discovered that the American traveller was not like the British. He was more forthright, less concerned with culture and less prepared to overlook deficiencies in hotel and transport services, nor was he prepared to do as Rome did in Italy or anywhere else. He demanded iced water, eggs, pancakes, ham and steaks for breakfast and then complained because these were charged to his bill. Exasperated, Cook talked about his customers' 'high airs and tall talk'.

Mark Twain himself wrote about his fellow Americans who 'talked very loudly and coarsely and laughed boisterously where all others were quiet and well behaved'.

The problems of the first few years were soon overcome as the tourists became used to European ways and Europeans became accustomed to American demands.

Summer excursions up the St Lawrence were popular at the turn of the century but Canada took longer to become established as a tourist destination than did the United States.

The Union Pacific Railway opened up the tourist route to the West Coast (1885).

Many Cook's tourists were in educational or religious groups such as this Good Templars party, photographed in Zurich in 1897.

As with more recent cultural clashes between tourists and nationals of the host countries, the initial antagonism gave way to acceptance and in a few years to a deeper understanding.

Cook's relationship with Jenkins went from euphoria to despair, however. The Cooks, with their long and arduous experience of building up the business, found it difficult to accept their new partner's profligate ventures. Jenkins founded an *American Excursionist*, wrote up the Cook tourist system in great bursts of hyperbole and spent money in an expansive way on such ventures as the Cook Pavilion at the Centennial Exhibition of 1876. Soon, John Mason Cook was writing to ask him to

THE POPULAR ROUTE TO THE
GRAND TRUNK RAILWAY SYSTEM
WORLD'S FAIR
St. Louis, Mo., 1904
OPEN FROM APRIL 30th TO DECEMBER 1st.

Through fast trains from points in the East, including Boston, Portland, Quebec and Montreal. Also from New York, Philadelphia and Buffalo via Niagara Falls.

Stop-over allowed at any point in Canada, Niagara Falls, Detroit and Chicago.

Unexcelled roadbed.

Modern and up-to-date equipment.

Polite employees.

NIAGARA FALLS

For
Handsomely Illustrated
Descriptive Matter
apply to

G. T. BELL

General Passenger and
Ticket Agent

MONTREAL

GRAND TRUNK RAILWAY BRIDGE AT NIAGARA

The St Louis World's Fair was an event that encouraged tourism. The Cooks promoted the Grand Trunk Railway system in their *Travellers Gazette*.

account for his expenditure. Jenkins did not reply. John Mason, never a patient man, wrote him an ultimatum. 'Unless the whole of the A/c's are at once adjusted ... I shall be reluctantly compelled to place our cashier and receiver in your office to wind up the business.'

By 1878, Jenkins wanted to resign but John Mason Cook would not let him do so without a complete accounting's being carried out first. Jenkins' reply to that was to leave for a holiday in Europe with £3,000 drawn from the company. This was the final straw, and John Mason promptly wrote to all the Cook offices telling them not to receive Jenkins nor to pay his hotel vouchers.

On his return, Jenkins sued Cook for $50,000 damages on the grounds that John Mason's letter had ruined his European trip and that the money he had taken was in any case due to him. He also claimed that the growth of the Thomas Cook business in America was due largely to his enterprise.

Jenkins won his but the judge awarded him only six cents damages. There is little doubt that the quarrel was to some extent a matter of a clash of personalities. The Cooks had worked hard for their business and its success had only been achieved as a result of the dedication of the whole family. John Mason felt himself the heir and protector of the Cook success and no doubt he was worried about the expansionist approach that Jenkins used to develop the business in America. He knew that in the travel business the dividing line between success and failure was very fine indeed, as it still is, and he saw in Jenkins' strategy a recipe for disaster.

Taking the business in hand himself on Jenkins' departure, John Mason began to build it up until in the 1880s and 1890s the name Cook was as much a household word in the United States as it was in Britain.

There were tours to every part of America, tours for Americans to every part of the world and special European emigrant arrangements offering fares to Canada for £3 and to the United States for £2.16s. Sometimes these fares included a small plot of land on which to build a home and start a new life.

To mark the fact that the Company had become established in the United States, it had, while still led by Jenkins, participated in the great Centennial celebrations at Philadelphia in 1876. A quarter of a million people arrived on the first day to see this exhibition in celebration of Independence. To many of them the Cook pavilion, set

A traveller to the St Louis World Fair used this postcard advertising Cook's Nile Steamers to relay his impressions of the Fair.

64

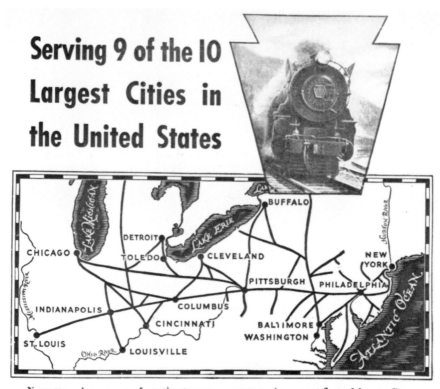

Serving 9 of the 10 Largest Cities in the United States

Continuing the tradition of comfort in railway travel, the Pennsylvania Railroad claimed to have the largest fleet of air-conditioned trains in the world in 1937—but in spite of such luxury a decade later the public were taking to the air.

No matter where you go from the steamer it is probable that you will take the Pennsylvania Railroad. Because it traverses the most thickly populated territories in America . . . its rail service is the most complete, most desirable and efficient on the North American Continent.

Whatever your itinerary; to Washington . . . New York . . . Philadelphia . . . Pittsburgh . . . Chicago . . . Detroit . . . Cleveland . . . Cincinnati or St. Louis . . . you will find at your service a great fleet of famous Pennsylvania Railroad flyers . . . completely air-conditioned for clean, quiet comfort at all seasons . . . conveniently scheduled . . . luxuriously appointed with the most modern types of all-steel train equipment.

The famous BROADWAY LIMITED between New York and Chicago heads the fleet. Of this great flyer it is truly said . . . "there is no finer train in America."

For advance information about trains, schedules, fares, etc., consult your nearest office of Thos. Cook & Son, Ltd., General Foreign Passenger Agents

Pennsylvania Railroad
The Largest Fleet of Air-Conditioned Trains in the World

in a garden and topped by a statue of Atlas and some vases, its doors guarded by two sphinxes (one of which collapsed under the weight of a lady weighing twenty stone), must have aroused nostalgia for the Europe from which they had emigrated.

The American business grew prodigiously after the celebration, and Cook's newly introduced system of 'checks' which he called Circular Notes was an instant success, as it provided the means of carrying money safely. The circular notes, which were an early form of traveller's cheque, had been introduced in 1873 in denominations of £5 and £10 and could be cashed at the growing number of hotels participating in the Cook system. When he introduced the cheque there were some two hundred hotels on Cook's lists. By 1876 the number had doubled, and by 1880 it was climbing rapidly towards a thousand. The Cook's tour system had hit gold, not only in America but all over the world.

Winter sports became a popular form of holiday between the wars and gave an impetus to the building of new resorts, with funiculars and cable cars to facilitate access to the slopes.

Winter Sports

COOK'S HANDBOOK 1935-6

CHAPTER FIVE

Around the World and After

While Cook was struggling to establish a business in the American market he was also looking eastward to Egypt and beyond. The opening of the Suez Canal in 1869 had greatly facilitated the passage to India and the Far East, and so, with eastward and westward expansion in mind, he now decided on the most ambitious Cook's Tour of all, a journey round the world. The tour was to begin with an Atlantic crossing on the most modern ship afloat, the *Oceanic*, and would then cross the great American Continent to San Francisco, where the party would take a ship to Japan, which had only recently been opened to westerners. Then via China, India and the Red Sea, the party would join up with the other Cooks Tours which were beginning to operate from London to Cairo.

There were only eleven people on the first round-the-world Cook's Tour in 1872, but they were a polyglot company representing the growing international appeal of the Cook system; among them were citizens of America, England, Scotland, Russia, Greece and Armenia.

As he travelled on his momentous voyage, Cook kept up a stream of articles for *The Times* newspaper in London in which he described the journey and his opinion of the countries he travelled through.

The Americans were courteous and he admired their habit of drinking iced water, but was repulsed by the 'admixture of strangers and sexes' in the sleeping cars, and the trains were slow. He was also upset by the treatment of immigrants. They were obliged to travel on special cars attached to freight trains and if found on a regular train were thrown off. 'Emigrants with children,' says Cook 'have to spend wearisome days and nights on hard boards with perhaps scanty food, before they reach their destination in the western states, where they are going to enrich railroad companies by the cultivation of their lands and the new territories of the states.'

The journey across the Pacific was tedious and, as he told his wife Marianne, to whom he wrote frequently, there were fifty cabin passengers aboard and the rest were steerage, mostly Chinese and Japanese who no doubt had been part of the labour force recruited to build the Transcontinental Railway.

Cook was amazed to discover that one of the Chinese emigrants had the bones of his father in his pillow case and was taking them back to his native land for burial. He was even more astonished when he arrived in Shanghai, which he found full of 'narrow, filthy and offensive streets and almost choking bazaars with pestering and festering beggars in every shape and hideous deformity'. The sight, sounds and smells soon drove him back into the compounds run by British, American and French traders, making a mental note not to take his tourists to the native city.

The contrast with Japan, which he had just visited, was too much. The Japanese had been courteous and clean and Cook's opinion was that 'Japan was a land of great beauty and fertility. The inhabitants and the government are rapidly transforming

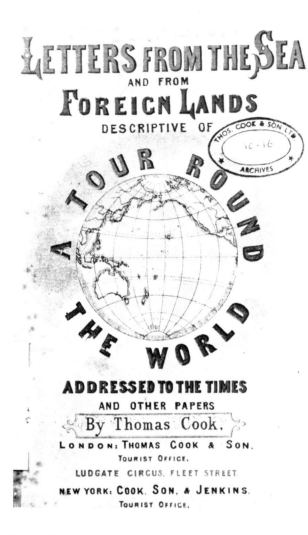

LEFT
The first conducted round-the-world tour took place in 1872–3 and, as he travelled with his party of ten, Thomas Cook reported it to *The Times*.

into enlightened, peaceful and cordial citizens.' He was particularly pleased to read that the 'trafficking in human bodies' was to cease, and that the prostitutes, singing and dancing girls, who were in virtual bondage to their employers for debts that they could never repay, were to be set free and that there were to be no complaints about money lent to them.

The employment of 119 Englishmen at the Imperial Court out of a total foreign staff of 214 also made him rejoice, for he could only believe that their influence would be to teach the Japanese how to adopt the ways of English gentlemen.

In India, Cook travelled 2,300 miles to Benares, Agra, Cawnpore, Lucknow, Delhi, Allahabad, Jubbulpore and Bombay, examining the hotels and railway systems and negotiating deals. He also found time to give talks, preach, and set up a library and, of course, to look after his tourists.

The party travelled in a railway carriage which was their home for three weeks and was attached to various trains as it went round India. A similar system for touring India is used today though, as in Cook's time, most of the Indian population still travel in crowded conditions in third-class carriages or on their roofs.

Ever alert to examples of intemperance, Cook was dismayed to find so much

While Thomas Cook was travelling round the world for real the fictional Phineas Fogg was doing so in the Jules Verne story serialised in a Paris newspaper.

Full details of the intended world tour appeared in *The Excursionist* of June 1872. The cost of the tour was to be 270 guineas.

COOK'S EXCURSIONIST AND TOURIST ADVERTISER, JUNE 24, 1872. 9

MR. THOS. COOK'S PROPOSED PERSONAL TOUR ROUND THE WORLD.

PRELIMINARY PROGRAMME.

At the close of the busy season of the last Universal Exhibition in Paris, in 1867, Mr. Cook intimated his intention of arranging in the following year for a second Tour to the United States, extending to California; and he also repeated an intimation, previously given, of his intention to make arrangements in the following autumn for a Tour to Egypt and Palestine. At that time the idea of going round to Egypt by way of China, or by Australia, had not formed a part of his plans. But the extraordinary facilities now offered by the steamboat arrangements of the Pacific, the Indian and the Red Seas, and the firm footing that Mr. Cook's Tourist arrangements have secured in the East, by a succession of several years of success, have led him to determine to offer his personal services to a Party that may be disposed to fall in with his arrangements.

To justify this great undertaking, it is necessary that there should be not less than ten travellers, and it is not desired to have more than twenty for the all-round trip. But for other sections, as far as San Francisco, or even New Zealand or Australia, or China or Japan, the numbers may be increased; and if there should be forty or fifty for the United States and California, there would be no difficulty in providing for them. We command Seven Lines of Ocean Steamers between Liverpool or Glasgow, and New York or Canada, and can furnish Single or Double Voyage Tickets for those points, the Return Tickets being good for Twelve Months. On the American Railroads any number of Passengers may be conveyed, to any distance between New York and San Francisco; and we shall not have difficulty in securing a liberal arrangement over the American Lines.

As Mr. Cook proposes to return by way of Egypt, he will arrange to see all that is practicable on the outward journey, calling at Niagara Falls, Chicago, the Mormon City of Salt Lake, and other intermediate places. Although but eighteen days may be actually required for travelling between Liverpool and San Francisco, there will be no difficulty in allowing, say twenty-five days extra for stoppages in America, if we get away from England by the first week in September.

The question most difficult to decide is, which route to take from San Francisco to India. The China route is the most expeditious, but we incline to the idea that most English Travellers would prefer to get glimpses of our own Colonies of New Zealand and Australia. We cannot, personally, go both ways, but it may be practicable for us to select the Australian route, and allow any who prefer it to go by the other route. Our object in issuing this preliminary programme is to elicit the desires of intending travellers, and then square our own course accordingly. Personally, we should certainly prefer to mingle with our own people to those with whom we could hold no conversation, however much we might wish to see them in their own countries. Nor would it be at all improbable that we might enlist in Australia travelling companions to accompany us to Egypt and Palestine. Our aim will be to get to Egypt about the beginning of the new year, so as to enable those who wish to go up the Nile to make that Trip before entering Palestine. But we shall not make either a Nile or Palestine Tour obligatory, but afford facilities for coming forward to Italy, France, and England, without making a lengthened stay in the East.

The All Round Tour will be divided as follows:—

I.—A Trip to New York for Single or Double Voyage.
II.—Through Tickets to Chicago, calling *en route* at Niagara Falls.
III.—Through Tickets for Single or Double Journey to California, calling at Salt Lake City.
IV.—Through Tickets from San Francisco to Japan, China, New Zealand, Australia, or India. This arrangement for India might be convenient for some who wish to see America *en route*.
V.—All Round the World, returning direct from Egypt by Brindisi, or other route to London.
VI.—Extensions of the Tour from Egypt to the First Cataract of the Nile, to Sinai, to Palestine, to Turkey and Greece; any, or all of these additions, with Italian arrangements as may be desired.

Under these half-dozen heads may be embraced a great variety of travelling details, which can be met by special arrangement.

In quoting Fares and other expenses, we can show them with a near approximation to accuracy. It is an easy matter to quote figures for certain defined and undeviated routes, and it is equally easy to name a lump sum of £500, more or less, allowing ample and unestimated margin for many unforeseen contingencies; but approximately correct figures lie somewhere between certain advertisements which have appeared in the public prints of this and other countries. We have tested two sides of the Circle, and know pretty well what will be required between here and the Pacific, and are quite ready to fix actual sums for Egypt, the Nile, Palestine, &c., or the direct journey home. The charges between San Francisco and Suez have been well considered and estimated; and they are mainly covered by the Steamboat Fares, which include Provisions—"wine and strong drink" excepted.

An esteemed friend, just returned from India, confirms our impressions that we shall be in India at the very best time of the year—in the cool season; and the arrangement will harmonize most admirably with the proper season for our usual Eastern Tours.

The foregoing intimations will serve for a starting-point of enquiry for those who are really desirous of entertaining the subject, and for others who might be disposed to raise questions for amusement or curiosity, we have nothing more to add at present. A large circle of old friends of our Excursions and Tours will watch with friendly interest the progress of these arrangements, and their good wishes will accompany us all the journey through. Already several are anxiously waiting for full particulars, and there is every prospect that our minimum of numbers will be exceeded.

The following Table has been arranged to show, as soon as possible, the time required, the distances to be traversed, and the cost of the several Divisions of the Tour. Slight alterations may have to be made in some of the details, but it is believed that the Estimates are substantially correct.

APPROXIMATE ESTIMATE OF TIMES, DISTANCES, & FARES.

From LIVERPOOL. Three or Four Days longer from Glasgow.	TIME of Travelling.	DISTANCE.	FARES. SINGLE.	FARES. DOUBLE.
	DAYS.	MILES.	GUINEAS.	GUINEAS.
New York	10	3,000	15 to 20	20 to 30
Chicago	12	3,890	20 to 25	....
San Francisco	18	7,400	48	72
Honolulu (Sandwich Islands)	28	9,200	52	....
Auckland (New Zealand)	42	13,100	78	....
Sydney (Australia)	47	14,370	83	....
Melbourne „	50	14,630	87	....
Galle (Ceylon)	71	19,300	105	....
Calcutta (India)	78	20,615	110	....
Bombay „	80	21,015	117	....
Suez (Egypt)	94	24,615	Round Fares [illegible]	....
Alexandria „	95	24,830		....
Brindisi (Italy)	98	25,680		....
London	102	26,880		....

The Fares from Glasgow, by the Anchor Line, to New York, will be £5 less to all points than the above quotations.

Return Tickets to New York, Chicago, or San Francisco, will be good for 12 months, allowing breaks of journey at all chief places.

The Fares quoted above do not include deviations over branch or connecting lines—say, to Salt Lake City, &c.

To the San Francisco time it is proposed to add 25 days for intermediate stoppages, and the Fare, including all Hotels, Railway Refreshment Rooms, Palace Saloon, and Sleeping Berths on the Railways, will be 80 guineas for the single journey.

These additions to the other quotations, as far as Bombay, will amount to 37 guineas in each case, and one guinea for every day on land above 25 days.

The Fares for the Round Tour, as indicated above, returning to London from Brindisi by any of the three routes—the Brenner; Naples or Ancona, and the Mont Cenis Tunnel; including sixty days' Hotel accommodation on land, in America, New Zealand, Australia, Ceylon, India, Egypt, and the Continent, with Palace Car Saloon and Sleeping Berths on the American Railways,

TWO HUNDRED AND SEVENTY GUINEAS.

If more than sixty days are required on land, one guinea per day to be paid extra for all additional time.

The Fares do not, in any case, include Wines, Beer, or Spirits.

All the arrangements are for First Class Travelling on sea and land, and for First Class Hotels.

Parties may be taken up or set down at intermediate places by the way, at proportionate Fares.

If any choose to leave Mr. Cook, or so to deviate as to render it impracticable for him to contract expenses at hotels, &c., an allowance of a guinea per day will be made for the time they are absent from him.

The Berths on the Steamers are for Ladies or Gentlemen, occupying Single Berth in a General Cabin. Married Couples occupying Reserved Cabins will have to pay about 20 per cent. extra on the Steamers.

An Extra Trip up the Nile to the First Cataract and back to Cairo, by Steamer, will be £44.

An Extra Trip from Cairo to Port Said and Jaffa, and for 30 days in Palestine to Beyrout, returning to London from thence by Austrian Lloyd's Steamer to Brindisi or Trieste, and thence by Rail, &c., all charges of horses, tents, provisions, &c., included—50 to 75 guineas, according to numbers of party, route, &c.

An Extra Trip from Suez to Sinai and back, including camels, tents, provisions, and all Dragoman's charges—if three persons or more, 25 guineas each.

Arrangements can also be made for extra time and détours in Italy, Switzerland, and France, at slight additional charges for travelling, with Hotel Coupons for time above 60 days on land, as previously shown.

DEPOSITS

May now be paid on any of the above Tours, say of the amount of 10 per cent. on the quotations, which will be returned to the depositors, less 10 per cent. on the amount deposited, if notice is given fifteen days previous to the timed fixed for departure. All Through Fares to be paid five days before the time of departure.

Although Mr. Cook has resolved to go by New Zealand and Australia, if any choose to go by China and Japan, arrangements can be made for their separation from the party between San Francisco and Egypt, or between San Francisco and Calcutta, the Fares for that route being about £10 more than by Australia.

THE NEXT TOURS TO THE EAST,

Going the direct way to Egypt, will be fully advertised when our Dragoman arrives, shortly after the 1st of July. In the meantime we repeat the notice that Alexander Howard, our chief Dragoman, from Beyrout, will conduct a party, in the autumn, through Italy, to Athens, Constantinople, Smyrna, Beyrout, over the Lebanon to Baalbec, and to the Cedars if desired; from Baalbec to Damascus, and from thence through Galilee and Samaria, to Jerusalem, the Jordan, the Dead Sea, Hebron, Bethlehem, Jaffa, &c.; and to Egypt, for the Nile, or for Sinai.

That arrangement will be followed by others for the months of January and February, reversing the arrangements by going first to Egypt, and from thence from South to North of Palestine and the Lebanon, in accordance with the natural course of the season. Mr John M. Cook and Assistants will superintend the arrangements, and accompany the travellers in January and February, 1873.

drunkenness in India and even more shocked to discover that 'the sale of drink is one of the easiest, the idlest and most productive ways of getting money, and English merchants ply the business with extraordinary zeal'.

The unacceptable face of the Empire did not discourage Cook however; he saw in this great spread of British influence nothing but good and a commercial opportunity that opened up undreamt-of new worlds to conquer.

On his return to London after nearly a year of travelling, Cook received a bad shock. Having left his son in charge of the Fleet Street office at a time when it was burdened with interest charges on the money he had borrowed, he found that the debts had all been cleared. Instead of being pleased, Cook was furious; later John Mason wrote, 'My father said he would not believe it possible but flew into a passion and declared that I had either robbed him or somebody else to enable the money to be paid.' This was the beginning of a quarrel which was to last nearly twenty years and which led to Thomas Cook's semi-retirement from the business.

Though Cook had been succeeded by his son as the head of the business, the public were not aware of the rift between father and son. The company continued to be called Thomas Cook and Son, and Cook's Tours went on from Strength to strength.

John Mason was an active and determined man and though a Temperance supporter, did not let ideologies stand in the way of business. He was, in fact, a typical late Victorian businessman, concerned with what was right and just within the ethos of his kind, and convinced that God, Queen and Empire were more or less one and the same thing.

His sons, Frank, Ernest and Thomas now joined the business and fulfilled special roles under their father's tutelage. By 1880, the three men had managed to set up sixty offices and agencies across the world and persuaded 500 hotels to accept the Cook coupons. In five years more, they had doubled these numbers and were soon able to list over a thousand hotels which found it indispensable to their business to belong to the Cook system.

The Excursionist and Exhibition Advertiser of 1851 led to a series of editions in French, German and Spanish, with special editions for Australia, Malaya, the Far East and America.

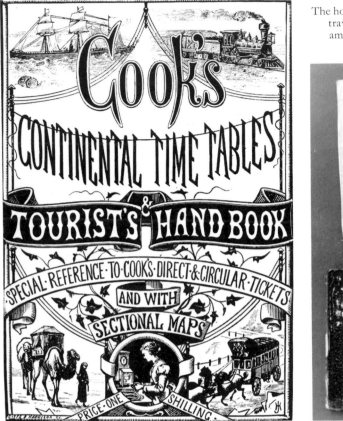

ABOVE
This timetable was launched in 1873 and has continued publication uninterrupted, except for the war years, to the present day. It now has a companion—the *Overseas Railway & Bus Timetable*.

As the business grew, the Cooks needed to appoint thoroughly reliable men to run their offices overseas. Among them are some whose names appear repeatedly in correspondence and in the pages of *The Excursionist*, which was now published in French, German, Indian, Australian, and Oriental editions. Etzenberger, the Cooks manager in Egypt was one of these, and another was Ripley, a fellow Temperance supporter who became one of John Mason's trusted lieutenants.

In an age when it took time to travel from one part of the Cook world network to another, trust was indispensable, as was total obedience to the method of operations laid down by John Mason.

Sending his son Frank to superintend the first offices in Australia at the time of the Melbourne Centenary, John Mason prepared a paper on the accounts system. Each sub agency was to report to a main regional office which then reported to Melbourne. The accounts were to be kept separately for Ticket sales, European tickets, Circular Notes, Commissions due, Australian Railway ticket sales, Hotel Coupons, Commissions payable to agents, Trade accounts covering rent, light, printing and taxes, and there was to be another account for the Australian *Excursionist* magazine.

To keep an eye on the movements of their tourists and to provide them with help, the Cooks set up a system of interpreters in the main cities and transfer points: Paris, Brindisi, Turin, Venice, Marseilles, Rome, Naples, Constantinople, Athens, Alexandria, Jaffa, Beirut and New York were the first to have those men in blue uniforms with gold buttons who stood so solidly and reliably as the Rock of Ages at all places where tourists milled about in helpless anxiety, waiting for help and guidance.

Before opening up their business in Australia, the Cooks had been given an opportunity to start up their business in India by the chance approach of the Italian railways.

'In order to carry out a special contract we have entered into with the Italian Government Railway Adminstration to act in India,' wrote John Mason, 'we have established a branch office in Bombay.' This was soon followed by one in Calcutta and another in Delhi.

By this arrangement the Cooks now began to offer trips to India via Brindisi, using the P&O (Peninsular and Orient) Line at fares of £74. 2s. 1od. for first class

RAILWAY ACCOMMODATION and WAGONS-LITS.
GENERAL PHRASES

YHHRE	... Gent(s) place(s) to be secured in Sleeping Car, Lits-Salons, Couchettes or 1st class seats, in this order of preference (on ...) (for ...)
YHHSU	... Lady(ies) place(s) to be secured in Sleeping Car, Lits-Salons, Couchettes or 1st class seats, in this order of preference (on ...) (for ...)
YHHUZ	Married couple(s) places to be secured in Sleeping Car, Lits-Salons, Couchettes, or 1st class seats, in this order of preference (on ...) (for ...)
YHHVO	Drawing Room to be reserved (to)
YHHYI	Compartment (Stateroom) to be reserved (to)
YHHZY	Section (upper and lower berth) to be reserved (to)
YHIAB	
YHIBR	
YHICG	
YHIDW	Smoking compartment (if possible)
YHIEL	Non-smoking compartment (if possible)
YHIFA	Ladies compartment (if possible)
YHIGQ	Facing Engine (if possible)
YHIHF	Back to Engine (if possible)
YHIIV	Corner seat(s) facing Engine (if possible)
YHIJK	Corner seat(s) back to Engine (if possible)
YHILP	Corner seat(s) vis-à-vis (if possible)
YHIME	Corridor seat(s) facing Engine (if possible)
YHINU	Corridor seat(s) back to Engine (if possible)
YHIOJ	Corridor seat(s) vis-à-vis (if possible)
YHIPZ	Window seat(s) facing Engine (if possible)
YHIQO	Window seat(s) back to Engine (if possible)
YHIRD	Window seat(s) vis-à-vis (if possible)
YHIST	
YHITI	
YHIUY	
YHIVN	
YHIWC	
YHIXS	**Absolutely** essential
YHIYH	A small table essential
YHIZX	Lower berth preferred
YHJAA	Lower berth essential
YHJEK	Upper berth
YHJHE	Compartments communicating if possible
YHJIU	Compartments communicating essential
YHJLO	In centre of car (carriage) if possible
YHJOI	In centre of car (carriage) essential
YHJPY	As near as possible to Restaurant Car
YHJUX	
YHJYG	
YHKCE	**Train** No ...
YHKDU	Train leaving at ...
YHKEJ	
YHKGO	
YHKIT	**Will pay** to your office
YHKJI	Will pay to the Conductor
YHKKY	
YHKOH	
YHKUW	We are issuing voucher, passenger will call for bulletin
YHKWA	Send bulletin to Conductor, amount paid here
YHKYF	Places asked for by ... office, to whom we cannot give satisfaction: please telegraph them direct
YHLAZ	... office has passed your application on to us
YHLBO	In reply to your application sent to (... office) as they have sold all their places, we are reserving ...
YHLEI	
YHLFY	
YHLIS	Do everything possible: we **commend** them to you
YHLOG	Recommended by the Direction Générale
YHLRA	**Release** to us all your places
YHLUV	
YHLYE	
YHLZU	**Reply** by letter
YHMAY	We await reply to our request (of ...)
YHMEH	
YHMIR	

Keeping in touch with the world network of offices was a difficult business. The installation of cables made communication easier, and Cook's developed their own code.

The colourful hotel labels which travellers pasted on their luggage advertised both the hotels and the fact that the owner of the luggage was a member of an élite.

OPPOSITE
Italian and French transatlantic shipping advertising had a stylish manner suited to the sophistication of its customers.

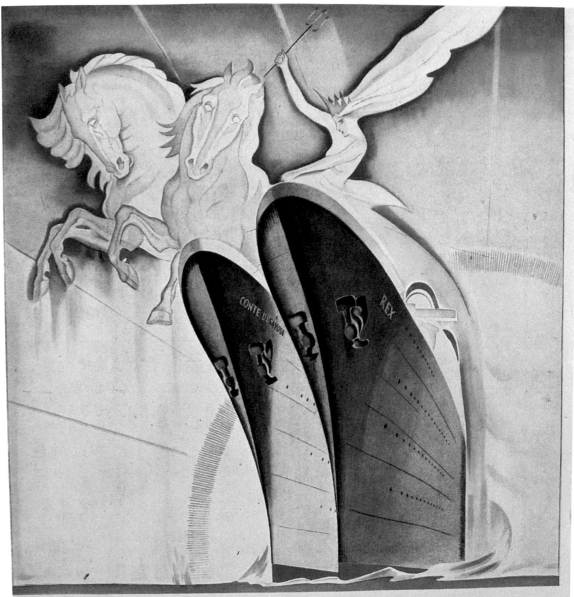

LEAVING LONDON DECEMBER 22nd, 1939
and MARSEILLES DECEMBER 30th, 1939

The thousands of civil servants, military personnel and merchants who travelled to India formed a good base on which Cook's could build their business. The tourist literature played up the colour and pageantry of the country.

Tiger hunting was the Indian Government equivalent of the wild game safaris that the Cooks arranged in Africa for the select few.

The Viceroy of India encouraged John Mason Cook to arrange tours to Britain for Indian princes, and Cooks opened a special department to deal with their huge parties, which included wives, children, concubines, court attendants and sometimes even sacred cows.

Tourists lived like maharajahs in hotel palaces like the Taj.

ABOVE
The Kuala Lumpur—
Singapore Express was
luxurious, complete with
sleeping and buffet cars. It
provided transport from
Penang to Singapore.

With the introduction of the
internal combustion engine, a
ride through the Malayan
jungles became a thrilling
tourist excursion.

COOKS

INTERNATIONAL

FREIGHT SERVICE

MERCHANDISE, BAGGAGE, HOUSEHOLD OR
PRIVATE EFFECTS. MOTOR CARS. DOGS
& OTHER LIVE STOCK TRANSPORTED
GOODS STORED
INSURANCES EFFECTED
INFORMATION & RATES ON APPLICATION

LEFT
Queen Victoria asked
Thomas Cook to arrange for
the shipping of some of her
cattle to the Vienna
exhibition in 1873. This
prompted the introduction of
Cook's Freight Service.

OPPOSITE
The Golden Arrow stood for
smartness, and *Wagons-Lits*
were adept at projecting
this image.

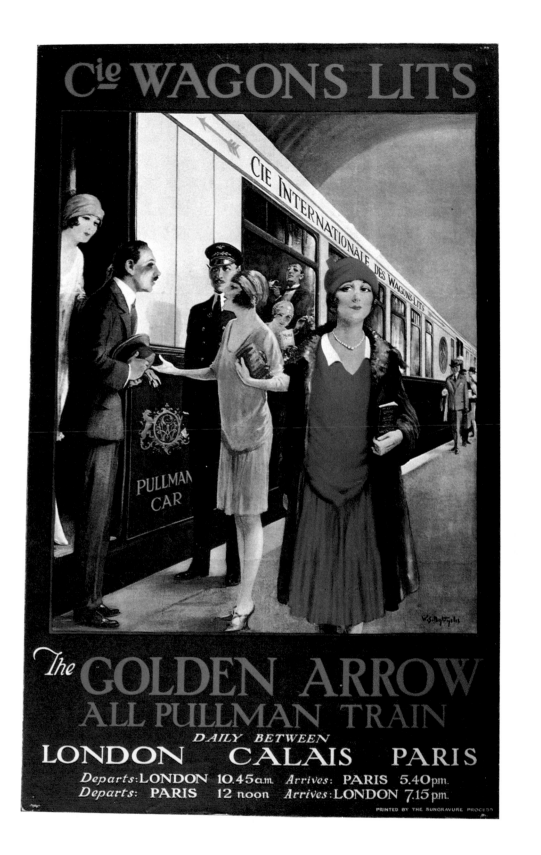

Japan was a popular holiday country especially with American tourists.

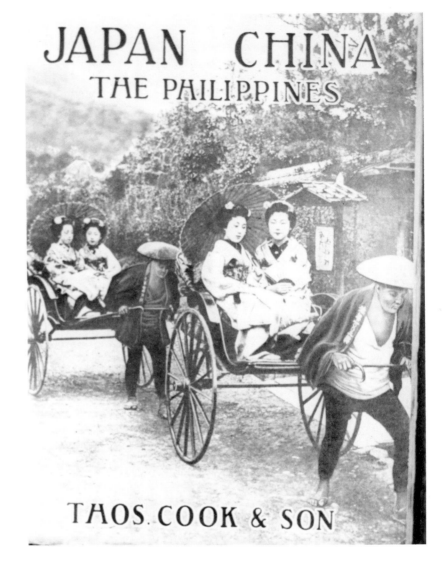

JAPAN CHINA
THE PHILIPPINES

THOS. COOK & SON

and £40.0s.11d. for second. To go all the way by steamer cost exactly £68. The Cooks also developed a hotel coupon system for India based on a 6s.9d. charge for room and breakfast at hotels with such gloriously English names as the Esplanade, the Great Western, the Apollo Bunder, Victoria Terminus and many others.

As the new Indian offices were opened, the Cooks grew close to the British colonial officials there, arranging travel for the increasing number of civil servants and army personnel who were pouring into the new jewel which Disraeli had presented to his sovereign.

India was the setting for one of the most extraordinary series of Cook's Tours ever devised. In 1885 John Mason Cook was requested by the Governor General Lord Dufferin to interest himself in the traffic of Moslem pilgrims to Mecca. This religious pilgrimage, which all Moslems felt obliged to undertake once in their lifetime, gave vast opportunities for sharp practice to what John Mason later called 'crimps, low lodging-house keepers and sharpers'.

As in most parts of the tourist world, in Japan there was no shortage of servants to attend to one's comfort.

Geishas were one of the romantic attractions of Japan. Here they are described rather mundanely as tea-house girls.

Tea-House Girls

The poor pilgrims who had saved up for years to pay for their passage from Bombay to Jeddah on the Red Sea, the disembarkation point for Mecca, were victims of disease, starvation, robbery and assault even before they arrived at Bombay, where they were subjected to further harassment by ships' agents. 'Eventually,' as someone engaged in the business explained to John Mason, 'a certain day is announced for embarkation . . . they all try and board at once . . . some are crushed to death.' The ships' holds were crammed with pilgrims and there were no toilet or washing facilities. Those who did not get below were often washed overboard once the ship was at sea. 'During the whole time the hatches are battened down and the shouting, screaming, and groaning are sickening,' a captain of one of the ships transporting pilgrims wrote to *The Times*.

John Mason and his sons worked continuously for several months to try and put some order into this business, but they were obstructed by those who had an interest in the traffic. In 1893 the enmity of these had grown so powerful that John Mason was asked by the government to resign the work. Like his father, John Mason hit back when attacked, and he wrote a long paper on the subject, the outcome of which was that the British government asked him to turn his mind to encouraging the local princes of India to visit Britain and thus strengthen their links with the Empire.

The focus of this operation was to be the great Colonial and India Exhibition in Exhibition Road, London in 1886. The Cooks created a special department called 'Indian Princes' and set about serving the richest and most demanding Cook's Tour customers that it had ever been their fortune to deal with.

Accustomed to an autocratic way of life, the princes were totally unaware of the limitations of travel in western Europe, and by their demands proved that almost everything is possible if one is determined enough.

Expecting to have to cope with similar special requirements to those of their more distinguished customers, among whom were members of the European nobility, the Cooks actually found themselves having to hire entire trains, ships and hotels to accommodate the courts of the Maharajahs, who thought nothing of travelling with wives, concubines, children, courtiers, pet tigers, sacred cows, elephants and even artillery.

Having succeeded in satisfying their travel requirements for the Exhibition, the Cooks gained a new and loyal clientele, until Indian Independence brought to an end their profligate way of life.

From this time until 1975, the Cooks adopted the telegraphic address 'Armagence' for all their banking communications. The telegraph was a boon to the Cooks' expanding empire, making it easier to maintain control of the far-flung offices. They created a code for the most frequent messages that had to be transmitted: *Addict* meant 'gents berth on a P&O steamer; *Adder* was a 'lady's berth on P&O'. Berths on other steamers were described as *Adhesive*; *Adult* was an order to 'secure any berth that is going'. *Candour* was a 'request for a single room'; *Dairy* meant 'Send a man to meet me', and *Infatuate* signified that there was 'no accommodation available'.

Running a world-wide business became increasingly difficult and even the entire Cook family was not large enough to cope with all the demands on them. Although they all travelled continuously, local managers became essential. Not all of them were good and even the good ones made mistakes, but John Mason ruled them with a rod of iron. His correspondence reveals his dictatorial style.

There had been some confusion over the payment of the bill of a Captain Romilly with no record of its settlement in Cairo or London. 'This,' wrote John Mason Cook to his accountant Faulkner, 'shows a want of business system.' Weeks later another letter to Faulkner refers to a loss in Banking and Exchange business for which John Mason wanted an explanation. 'I do not mean a rambling letter, but I want a tabulated account showing the date of purchase, whom they were purchased from, the date of the sales or commissions to America and the dates of any correspondence.'

The size of the business also made it more vulnerable to threats from its employees. On one occasion the guides employed in the Middle East, called dragomans, demanded an increase in pay. John Mason's response was instant and definite. 'I remember that I told you clearly and distinctly that I could not think of advertising such extortionate charges. I have not lost sight of the fact that there are only two or three good dragomen [sic] in the country but if there were only one I would not allow such fares to be advertised by us.'

LEFT
The exploration of Africa by Livingstone, Stanley, Speake and others fired the public imagination, and there was increasing interest in tourism there after 1900 when the Cooks opened their Cape Town office.

The Victoria Falls vied with Niagara as a tourist 'must'. In 1908 it cost £24 to go there from Durban and this included transport, meals and accommodation.

The problems mounted: dishonest employees, hoteliers who tried to perusade clients to book direct, steamship and railway companies who tried to set up in competition, bona fide competitors like Henry Gaze who wrote a booklet alleging that the Cooks' claims were untrue and that he (Gaze) was the pioneer in Middle East travel; these were typical of the times.

On the whole, though, the problems that arose as the company grew were compensated for by the increase in profits. These were particularly good where the Cooks had an exclusivity, as in the Nile steamer business. A profitable business attracted others into it, however, and encouraged principals to set up on their own to avoid paying the Cooks commission. It was all a question of whether the marketing and promotional expertise of the Cooks was able to produce more sales than a hotelier, shipping or railway company could do for itself.

In the early years and even after Thomas Cook moved to London, the business was one that could be dealt with from one office, for the people who travelled were relatively few and since there was no other way for them to obtain Circular Tickets, Hotel Coupons, and all the other pieces of paper that Cook invented, they were obliged to deal with the main office.

RIGHT
Australia was included in the early World Tours and later, in 1889, the Cooks published a book of advice to travellers to the Pacific Continent.

BELOW
The cover of the *Oriental Travellers' Gazette* summed up all the exotic character of Cook's Tours even if Victoria Station, Bombay did look rather like St Pancras.

ABOVE
The Cooks had offices in Shanghai, Tientsin, Peking, Kobe and Hong Kong during the 1930s, when this first China air tour brochure was issued.

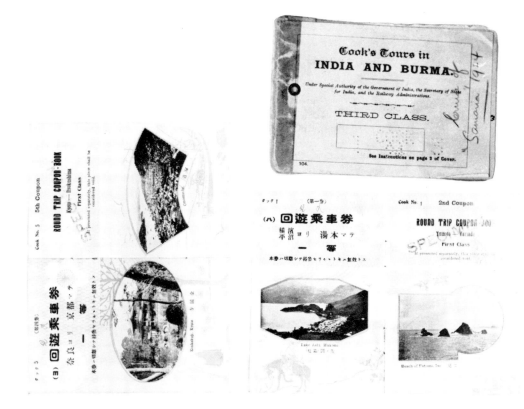

Japanese round trip ticket booklets, the Oriental equivalent of the Circular ticket, and (top) an India and Burma railway tour ticket.

There had been competitors, of course, people like Joseph Crisp of Liverpool, who as early as 1844 had made an agreement with the Grand Junction and the London and Birmingham Railways, and Henry Gaze who had also started in 1844 and had followed a parallel path to the Cooks but with less success.

After the 1880s, the Cooks could hardly handle more business and this left room for newcomers, especially in the British and European market. One of these was the Dean and Dawson company, later to become a Cook subsidiary. This company had been started by Joseph Dean and John Dawson, who were both in the railway agency business, and therefore appreciated the need to have as many ticket sales points as possible at a time when the idea of travel was spreading through society. Inevitably, they also entered the tour business, following the pattern set by Thomas Cook, and took some workers' groups of considerable size to Paris.

John Frame was another, who, motivated like Cook by the ideals of Temperance, began to organize trips abroad. Yet another was Henry Lunn, though he later thought it had been a mistake to try and compete on the popular level with Cook.

In America, American Express, who more recently have entered the field of travel in a big way, were not interested in the 1880s and 1890s; they were in the money and freight business and their President, William Fargo, said so flatly: 'There is no profit in the tourist business as conducted by Thos. Cook & Son and even if there were, this company would not undertake it.'

In fact, there was a good deal of profit for the company to win during what came to be called the *Belle Epoque*, and a beautiful enough epoch it turned out to be for the Cook family. They were able to realize some two million pounds when they retired from the business in the period between the two World Wars.

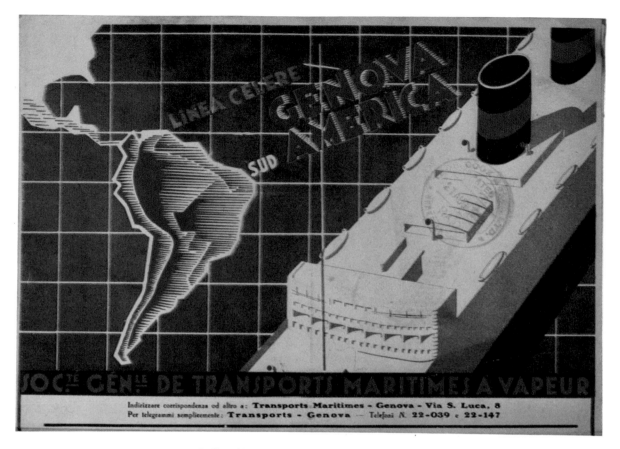

Italian shipping lines had traditional links with
South America, owing to the large Italian
emigrant population there.

OPPOSITE

A superb example of travel poster art
unfortunately now rare in a business that,
despite its opportunities, tends to produce
rather mundane advertising material.

CHAPTER SIX

The Gateway to the Empire

The opening of the Suez Canal in 1869 marked a new era of Imperialism. Egypt, in the hands of a decaying Turkish Empire, was ready for a new master, and all the European powers as well as Russia had their eyes on this strategic gateway to the East. With the French and the Prussians on the verge of the 1870 war and the Russians not able to challenge British seapower, it was natural that Egypt should come under British influence and later a Franco-British control.

Thomas Cook quickly consolidated his position as a pioneer in the area and soon dismantled all opposition. He was even accused by his competitor, Henry Gaze, of having stolen the latter's best dragomans. Within months of his first trip in 1869 Cook had further conducted tours and ticket systems working.

The best and most economical route to Egypt was across Europe by train to Brindisi and thence by steamer to Port Said. Cook offered this trip for 150 guineas and the public flocked to his offices. He was on to a good thing, for there was a steady traffic of military and civil service personnel to draw on. These were people who were en route or returning from India and the East and who welcomed a break during which they could see the monuments of Egypt which were attracting so much attention through the work of British archaeologists. And Cook could also rely on numbers of British tourists, prepared to make a journey specially to see the wonders of the new tourist country.

A Cook visit to the Middle East generally included a tour of the Holy Land, a region that lay close to Thomas Cook's heart because of its religious connotations. The problem as far as tours were concerned lay in the fact that there were virtually no hotels and none of the means of transport that he usually relied on.

With typical ingenuity and determination Cook set about creating the transport and the accommodation his parties would require. He organized what amounted to a luxurious army camp for parties of between thirty and forty tourists. This caravanserai moved about the deserts of Palestine served by an army of muleteers, servants and guards led by the masterful dragomans who administered the camp with a firm and authoritative hand. There were usually two of these as well as Cook or one of his family with each party and they commanded some twenty servants.

The inventory of camp equipment used on these desert expeditions generally included: eleven sleeping tents, two dining saloons, one cooking tent, thirty-five saddle horses, forty-two pack horses and mules, and fifteen asses.

The large number of pack animals was necessary because of the vast quantity and range of material and provisions Cook thought it essential to have to ensure that his tourists felt comfortable and safe. Most of these came from quiet, middle-class urban backgrounds, and travelling across limitless deserts far from civilization must have raised some fears in their minds; Cook was determined that they should suffer neither fear nor discomfort.

The Cooks arrived in Egypt
in 1869 and set up an office in
the grounds of Shepheards
Hotel. ·

BELOW
Shepheards Hotel was the
centre of social life in Cairo.

SOUTH AFRICA TOURS

SILAS

FOR FULL PARTICULARS APPLY TO

THOMAS COOK & SON,
LIMITED

Bask in Sunny

JAMAICA
B.W.I.

The
All-the-Year
HOLIDAY COUNTRY

Australia
JAVA
SINGAPORE
Service

Time Table
1939
BURNS PHILP LINE

Brochures of various
companies with whom Cooks
dealt.

Trips up the Nile were one of the major attractions of an Egyptian holiday. The Cooks became the owners of a large flotilla of steamers and dahabeahs, vessels for private parties. (c. 1890).

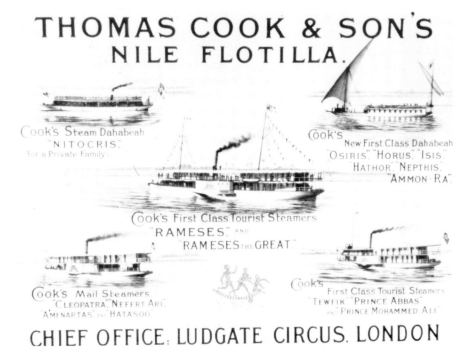

THOMAS COOK & SON'S NILE FLOTILLA.

Cook's Steam Dahabeah
"NITOCRIS."
For a Private Family.

Cook's New First Class Dahabeah
"OSIRIS," "HORUS," "ISIS,"
"HATHOR," "NEPTHIS,"
"AMMON-RA."

Cook's First Class Tourist Steamers
"RAMESES," AND
"RAMESES THE GREAT"

Cook's Mail Steamers
"CLEOPATRA," "NEFERT ARI,"
"AMENARTAS" AND "HATASOO."

Cook's First Class Tourist Steamers
"TEWFIK," "PRINCE ABBAS"
AND "PRINCE MOHAMMED ALI."

CHIEF OFFICE: LUDGATE CIRCUS, LONDON

He carried iron bedsteads and mattresses for their comfort at night, tapestries and carpets for the tents, tables and chairs, and provisions which included porridge and eggs for breakfast.

The food that the Cooks served on these expeditions was something of a *tour de force*. Though it may not have lived up to the elegant standards of the Ritz, it made up in quantity for any defects in style. A typical dinner included hard-boiled eggs, cold chicken, lamb or mutton, or wild boar if one could be bought at the market, and a cooked pudding. These were accompanied by various vegetables and there was fruit and cheese for dessert as well as the pudding.

Nothing like a Cook's Desert Tour had ever been seen before and his customers soon publicized the excellence of his arrangements.

There were difficulties, of course. Sometimes the party had to camp outside the walls of cities in unsalubrious surroundings. Though it may not have been a real danger, there was also the ever-present threat of an attack by Arab bands. There is no record of a Cook's party being attacked, but Cook always made sure of employing members of the tribe whose territory the party was crossing, and he had scouts and watchdogs among the camp personnel.

The jokers among their Arab boy attendants sometimes caused uproar. They would prod the horses and mules carrying the travellers in a sensitive part of their anatomy, causing the animals to break into a wild gallop which usually ended by unseating the riders, upon which the mischievous boys would hurry up full of solicitude and earn themselves some baksheesh by helping the grateful traveller to his feet. At other times, the boys let the tents down in the mornings just as the ladies were dressing and there would be shrieks and embarrassment and more apologies and backsheesh.

On at least one trip there was tragedy. One of the tourists, a Mrs Samuels, died in

This extract from an illustrated map of the Nile, gives an idea of the immense variety of points of interest.

a remote desert convent and it needed all Cook's resourcefulness to ensure that she received a proper Christian burial in Jerusalem, although, according to Arab law, she should have been buried in the desert within twenty-four hours of her death.

A Miss Riggs of Hampstead, who was on the trip, later recounted how the Jerusalem burial was achieved. 'Arabs have a great superstition with regard to the dead, and as she was to be taken to Jerusalem to be buried, the natives were told that she was ill and she was packed up and carried, sitting in a palanquin.'

The ruse succeeded and Mrs Samuels was duly buried in Jerusalem at dead of night.

The Khedive of Egypt helped the Cooks to establish their business. He is seen here with his relations and attendants, and Thomas (Bert) Cook, wearing a bowler hat (*c.* 1910).

A Cook's party all ready for a sortie into the desert, including one member with shotgun (*c.* 1900)

These Cook's tourists were a tougher breed than those who patronized the French, Swiss, and Italian tours, and far removed again from the Scarborough trippers back home in England. From the letters and reports they left behind, they seem to have been a good-humoured and tolerant lot, though ready to react in righteous indignation at their visits to slave markets and dubious places of entertainment. Like the people who were building up the commercial Empire, they were interested in the places and people they visited. While holding firmly to their own principles and their own style of dress, even when the temperature was 100°F, they seemed on the whole to be free of the arrogance sometimes found among those

who had official positions in the Empire on which the sun never set.

Egypt was altogether different: here, the Cooks' Nile steamers were floating cocoons of middle-class security and comfort. The tourists could relax in luxury between bouts of going ashore, where they would be set upon by beggars, guides, camel drivers, donkey owners, souvenir sellers, salesmen of 'guaranteed' antiquities found in recently excavated tombs, and the plagues of flies and other abominations that filled the fetid air of Egyptian cities.

After he began operations in Egypt, John Mason Cook made arrangements to charter the government steamers and was soon advertising 'Steamboat trips up the Nile with the Khedive's authority—Exclusive arrangements'. His advertised fare from London to Cairo was £80 for first class and £75 for second. The price included fifteen days of Cook's European hotel coupons and ten days of Egyptian ones, as well as landing fees, hire of donkeys, guides and the payment of baksheesh.

Despite the protection provided by guides and company representatives from the importuning of those who saw in tourism a new means of earning a modest living, the Cook's tourists often had to fend for themselves with whatever means lay in their power or within reach. One lady describes her escort seizing a stick to keep baksheesh seekers at bay, while she held them off with an umbrella.

The tourists also did some damage though it is probable that the vandals were not the people travelling in Cook's conducted tours, but those travelling alone with the Cook's Circular Tickets. Wall paintings were often defaced and sometimes chunks of them were carved out of walls as souvenirs. There was little control over the ancient monuments that were constantly being discovered and, in fact, the museums themselves often sold pieces for which they had little use. There was a good trade in mummified cats, birds and other animals as well as in amulets and pottery. Whether all the treasures hawked about were genuine is questionable. The daughter of one Cook's manager stationed in Cairo told the author that her father had dug up a sarcophagus in his back garden and offered it to the British Museum

Many hands made a trip to Karnak light work for these five tourists (c. 1900).

95

This party called themselves the Nazareth Boys, although there were several women among them.

Cook's resthouse by the tomb of Queen Hatshephut (formerly Hatasu) provided refreshments and a refuge from the hot sun.

SERVICES DE
MM. Th. COOK ET FILS
en Egypte
et sur le Nil.

Cook's tourist literature appeared in many languages. Here the *Messieurs Cook et fils* advertise their Nile excursions to the French.

who turned it down. It was eventually disposed of through other channels to America.

The value of ancient ruins and *objets d'art* as a tourist attraction eventually came home to countries that were tourist destinations in the nineteenth century, and greater care was exercised in their conservation and protection. Today the visiting tourist is less likely to damage historic sights, for the public has been schooled to respect culture. On the other hand, awareness of the value of objects in such places as Pompeii seems to be encouraging vandalism and robbery of a more sophisticated nature.

In the 1880s everybody who wanted to be thought a *bona fide* traveller went to Egypt and the Nile and most of them travelled on a Cook's Tour. The leather-bound Cook's handbooks (presented to important passengers) included lists of passengers and today they read like a *Who's Who* of late nineteenth-century royalty, commerce and the arts. Beginning with the royal princes of Britain, the list goes through the Russian court from the Czar downwards, the German princes, the Royal families of Denmark, Brazil, Persia, Sweden, Prussia and Austria, Indian maharajahs, Nawabs, the Archbishop of Canterbury, and various celebrities of the day such as Randolph Churchill, Richard Chamberlain, Cecil Rhodes, Rider Haggard and Rudyard Kipling.

By the 1890s the Egypt business was booming. 1895 was a typical year. The Cooks had taken 742 Nile steamer bookings until March, which was the end of the season, as most tourists went to Egypt in winter to escape the rigours of the cold at home in Britain, Russia and America. The steamer's profit for the season had been £17,411.2s.4d. including profits from tourist passengers, local passengers,

The Cook steamers carried the Egyptian mail up and down the Nile. This is a steamer ticket to 'Assouan' from Cairo.

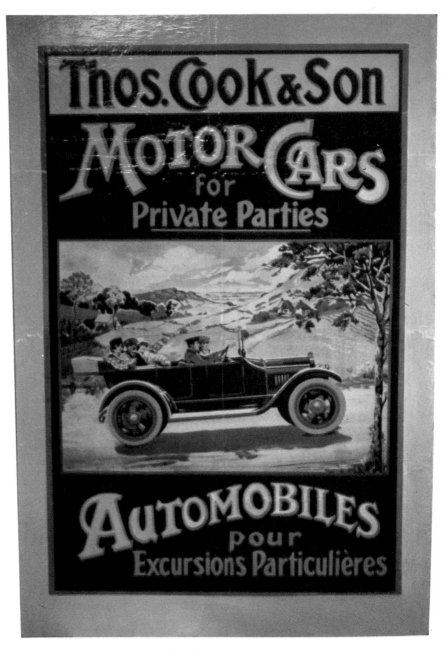

The Cooks introduced motoring holidays in 1903 and this
poster shows that they were still going strong in the 1920s.
Once motorists had learnt the way to tour the Continent
through Cook's, however, they began to go it alone, and this
holiday service was discontinued in the 1970s.

OPPOSITE
The new headquarters at Berkeley Street into which
Cook's moved in 1926 symbolized the stability and
continuity of the Company.

Palestine and Syria had been
visited by tourists since 1869
but as there were no hotels
the Cooks arranged a moving
encampment. By 1908 when
this brochure was issued there
was a choice of camping or
staying in hotels.

A Cook's office in Luxor
advertised, on the left of the
building, a reading room free
to all, with all the latest papers.

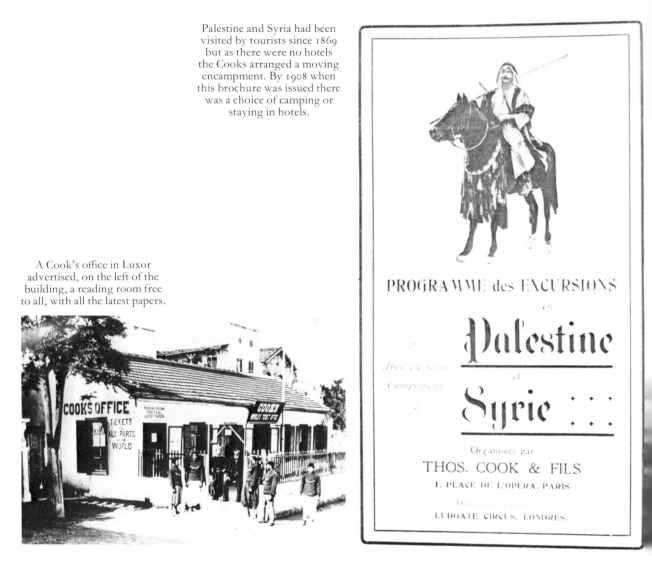

PROGRAMME des EXCURSIONS

Avec ou sans

Campement

Palestine

et

Syrie

Organisées par

THOS. COOK & FILS

1, PLACE DE L'OPERA, PARIS

LUDGATE CIRCUS, LONDRES.

Egyptian government mails (for the carriage of which Cook had the monopoly), and
the transport of Egyptian government personnel. Total expenses for the season
were in the neighbourhood of £12,000, so the company was doing well.

The Cooks' experience in Egypt included two remarkable events which are
probably unique in the history of tourism. The first occured in 1884 when General
Gordon, who had been sent to the Sudan to evacuate British residents, decided to
remain there in order to impose the Pax Brittanica on the country which was in the
throes of an uprising led by a religious leader, the Mahdi. Finding himself
surrounded by the Mahdi's followers at Khartoum, Gordon called for help but his
cries fell on deaf ears, for the British Government was not inclined to help someone
who had defied its orders. Thereafter he found himself in difficulties. Eventually,
driven by public clamour at its neglect of a national hero, the Government had to
act. Gathering a force together under General Wolseley, it ordered the Admiralty to
transport it up the Nile. The Admiralty soon found that the only British people who

knew about navigating the Nile were Thomas Cook and Son, so they were sent for to arrange a military Cooks Tour to Wadi Halfa, from where the army would march to Khartoum.

John Mason negotiated the terms, which included an agreement that he should receive an advance on his estimated cost so that he could start the operation. No money came and the plans were changed as the number of forces involved increased. John Mason who had a contract date to fulfil started things moving on his own account.

The original agreement was that he should move 6,000 men, 10,000 tons of stores, 12,000 tons of coal and 400 whaleboats by rail to Assiout and ship them by steamer to Wadi Halfa. The revised plan increased the quantity of men to 18,000 and the total tonnage of stores to 130,000. In addition, John Mason was asked to collect 50,000 tons of cereal in lieu of tax from fellahs [peasant farmers], on his way down river.

While the plans were being changed and renegotiated, the Mahdi was gathering his forces to attack Gordon. The situation was becoming critical and John Mason and his sons dedicated themselves to the task allotted to them, even without the promised advance, and began to ship coal from Britain. In the midst of this operation, they were asked by the Government to provide a guarantee that the work would be carried out.

A Colonel Furse, who served in the campaign, kept a diary in which he made some apt comments on the business of dealing with governments:

> John Mason was the real Quarter Master General of the expedition. To those with whom he came privately into contact he endeared himself by his amiable manners and readiness to answer every question put to him, which coming from a lot of griffs must at times have taxed his patience and equanimity. Here was the man who, in anticipation of work to be done on the Nile, had on his own hook sent out to Egypt, some thousands of tons of coal, was asked by the War Office when in the midst of his work for some guarantee for his fulfilment of his contract: this was really sweet, quite in keeping with the traditions of the Supply and Transport Dept. What a laugh we had about it when Cook told us.

Despite the dilatoriness and red tape, John Mason delivered the troops and supplies on time, though after the expedition had failed to relieve Gordon and Khartoum, there were some who wanted to lay some of the blame on his shoulders. Stung by the rumours, John Mason wrote to the Secretary of State for War demanding a statement on whether he had or had not fulfilled his contract. He received one on behalf of Campbell Bannerman, later the Liberal Prime Minister, in which it was agreed that 'considering the amount of organization required in arranging for the service, the difficulties of the Nile navigation and the great strain on local resources, he is of the opinion that great credit is due to you for the satisfactory way in which your contract was performed.'

The difficulties had certainly been much greater than John Mason had envisaged; there had been cataracts that even he was unaware of, wrecked boats, exhausted men who had to pull the boats over rapids, illness and five deaths. In addition, the Cook steamers were out of commission for the tourist season and though Cook was well paid for his work he might have earned more by serving his growing army of tourists.

An Australian brochure of
the 1920s.

Cook's were the first to offer
trips by air in 1919, and later
produced a special air
holiday brochure showing
scheduled services.

A 1903 party of tourists posing before the Dome of the Rock in Jerusalem.

The road to Damascus: those who were unable to ride were carried in the horse carriages seen in the background.

Another form of transport across the rough terrain of Palestine was the palanquin supported by mules.

This lady was on a shore excursion from a cruise ship in Morocco in the 1930s.

In 1889, when Kitchener's army set off to the Sudan to deal with the Mahdi once and for all (which he did at Omdurman in 1898), John Mason was once more put in charge of the transport. Once again, he had to face the usual problem of being undercut and even of having his ships requisitioned by the War Office. His reply to this was immediate.

'It would give us the greatest pleasure to meet the wishes of the Ministry, but we find it impossible . . . This vessel was handed over to us under our contract with the Egyptian Government for the performance of certain services which have been and are still being performed.'

John Mason continued to be in charge of the operation and his son Frank wrote to him from Luxor where he was overseeing the transport.

'Everything has gone off most successfully up to now. *Ramses the Great* left Balianah with two barges full of camels. *Ramses II* returned from Balianah with no damage done and is returned up river with more camels. Still 1,000 camels to be shipped.' Before this was done, however, the authorities had changed their minds yet again and the Cooks, eager to be rid of their onerous task, discussed whether this meant they could withdraw the steamers from military service and send them down to Cairo to be got ready for the tourist season.

By now, the Cooks were thoroughly in control of the Egyptian travel business and were the largest employers of labour in the country. As well as the staff at their offices and on their camping parties, they were responsible for the crews of the Nile Steamers; the people who cared for the beasts of burden; the men at the shipbuilding yards where they assembled the steamers brought piecemeal from Britain; and the

'Völker Europas wahret Eure heiligsten Güter'

Souvenir de Jerusalem

PAUL MICHEL & FILS BETHLEHEM PALESTINE

When Kaiser Wilhelm and his party went to the Holy Land with Thomas Cook in 1890 he had this postcard specially made to commemorate his visit.

fellahs in the tracts of land near Luxor and Assouan where they raised the chickens and grew the vegetables served to their tourists.

In Assouan a grateful people put up a hieroglyphic inscription to John Mason which read, 'King of Upper and Lower Egypt, John son of the sun, Cook and son, Lords of Egypt, Pharoah of the boats of the north and south, he fills the heart of his lady in the two countries. Her Majesty Queen Victoria, mistress of all lands, living for ever, he made the boats that brought the soldiers of Her Majesty to Wadi Halfa. He is the great man, lord of the Nile and gives bread to the mouths of the people of Thebes.' No wonder that a tourist wrote home, 'the arabs think that Cook is the king of England and carries on hostilities on his own account out of pure devilry and bloody-mindedness'.

The year after transporting Kitchener's army, John Mason was engaged with his son Frank in arranging a journey for another Imperial power, Germany. The Kaiser, grandson to Queen Victoria, was visiting the Holy Land which was still occupied by the Turks, and consolidating his country's understanding with them. The rivalry of the Imperial powers was bringing them all towards the confrontation of 1914 but at the time their moves must have seemed no more dangerous than moves on a chessboard. John Mason and Frank looked after their new client as assiduously as they did the British Royal Princes and the Archbishop of Canterbury. They were proud to have the Imperial flag over their tents, and even prouder when the Emperor decorated John Mason with the order of the Crown of Prussia and Frank Cook with the order of Jerusalem.

CHAPTER SEVEN

A Life on the Ocean Waves

The pioneers of steamship lines—Samuel Cunard, who was a Canadian; Edward Knight Collins, an American; and William Inman, a Liverpudlian who settled in America—earned their living in the early years of their shipping lines by carrying mail and emigrants. Their ships were packets designed not for comfort but speed, and most of the people who travelled in them did so from necessity rather than for pleasure.

Improvements in ship design in the nineteenth century, including screw propulsion and metal hulls, changed all this and before long the oceans of the world became yet another tourist playground.

The early leader in this new field of enterprise was William Inman, an associate of Collins, whose failure, caused partly by the fact that his wooden-hulled ships could not stand up to the heavy battering of the sea, convinced Inman that iron was essential. He bought the *City of Brussels* early in the 1850s and with this and other *City* ships carried on a lucrative trade in emigrants, whom he took across the Atlantic six hundred at a time, and in first class passengers for whom he provided luxurious accommodation. Inman's move began a battle for supremacy on the seas in which his and Cunard's companies were challenged by a number of other lines, including the White Star and Guion lines.

As mentioned earlier, Thomas Cook made his first transatlantic crossing in 1865, and very soon followed up his visit with a tour conducted by his son, and the establishment of a New York office. All the contending shipping lines were approached and Cook began to advertise American holidays in Europe, while also canvassing in the States for business from America to Europe.

The ships that began to develop after the Inman initiative were a quite different breed from those whose lack of confidence in steam was proclaimed by the sail that they still carried. Now the last vestige of sail and their masts and yards were discarded, and ships assumed a new and more rakish look, with superstructures which contained public rooms and promenades and the more expensive cabins.

The *Campania*, Cunard's answer to the Inman ships and to the White Star Line's *Teutonic* and *Majestic*, launched at the end of the 1880s, was a twin-screw, 12,500-ton ship with electric light and public saloons furnished like a grand hotel, even down to coal fires. To prevent time hanging heavily on the hands of its passengers, the ship had deck games, dances, competitions and gastronomic programmes that stretched throughout the day from fruit before breakfast to a final supper which followed a full dinner; altogether there were ten meals of one kind or another during the course of the day, and some passengers must have been grateful to get off the ship after ten days of this kind of gluttony.

Throughout the *Belle Epoque*, the steamship companies competed for the greatest speed and luxury, to such an extent that the national pride of all the nations

Dickens sailed to America in 1842 in the
steam packet *Britannia* which he found very
uncomfortable. This illustration appears in
his *American Notes*.

OPPOSITE
The P. & O. paddle steamer *Singapore* sets off
for South Africa. This is similar to the type
of steamer used for Atlantic crossings in the
middle of the nineteenth century.

LEFT
Cook's dealt with all the world's shipping
lines, as shown in this list published in 1900.

already jockeying for position in the European power stakes became involved.

The Germans arrived on the scene with the North German Lloyd and Hamburg-Amerika lines and in 1897 startled everyone by launching a giant ship of 14,350 tons appropriately named the *Kaiser Wilhelm der Grosse*. On her first voyage, the *Kaiser Wilhelm* took, and held for ten years, the Blue Riband of the Atlantic and within a year the company that owned her had taken over a quarter of the Transatlantic business.

Cunard, who had fallen behind in the race, now launched two ships which were to become unchallenged leaders in the Atlantic for over twenty years, the *Mauretania* and the *Lusitania*, both of which made their maiden voyages in 1907.

With a tonnage of 31,000 and a speed of at least 25 knots, they outstripped all their competitors and satisfied the national ego to an extent never achieved again. They were palatial, providing the leisured tourist with a style of living that even the best hotels could not offer. Public rooms were designed and furnished in the style of French *chateaux*, the dining rooms had huge domed ceilings, the state rooms were furnished and decorated in the styles of Adam, Sheraton and Chippendale, and the bars and smoking rooms reminded passengers of Italian *palazzi*.

Driven to reply to the Cunard challenge, the White Star Line produced the largest and safest ship in the world, the 46,328-ton *Titanic*, and when she struck an iceberg and sank on her maiden voyage in 1912, it was a portent not only for the whole world of shipping but for the leisured classes as well.

German national pride had meanwhile produced the 52,000-ton *Imperator* in 1912 and the *Bismark*, but were not to enjoy their supremacy for long since the ships were handed over to the British after World War I and rechristened *Majestic* and *Berengeria*; another huge ship, the 54,000-ton *Vaterland* went to the Americans and became the *Leviathan*.

When dealing with these, and other, smaller shipping companies, the Cooks' size and importance gave the company no little power in getting the terms they wanted. Wherever possible, they tried to obtain sole agencies in Britain and the United States. They achieved this in their 1880 contract with La Compagnie Generale Transatlantique, for instance, and with one Ernst George, a Lisbon shipowner, in 1885. This latter agreement is an interesting example of how comparatively simple it was for companies to do business in the less complicated business world of the

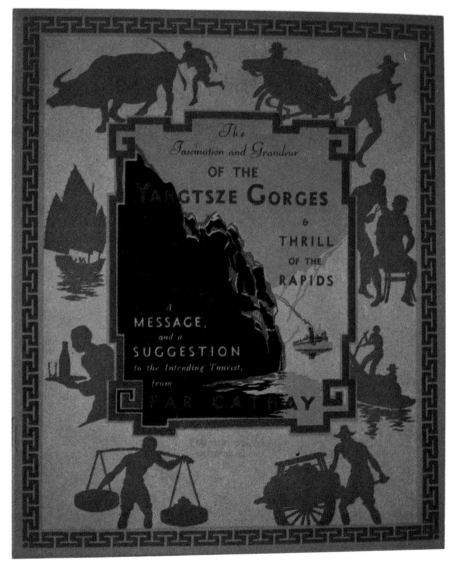

The Yangtse Gorges, recently featured in tours to
China, were also a place for the tourist in search of
away-from-it-all thrills in the 1930s.

OPPOSITE
An inked note on this Indian brochure reveals that in
the year 1935 Cook's sold 12,000 tours advertised in it.

INDIA

Ulysses S. Grant, a Cook's customer, is seen here, cigar in mouth, while on a round-the-world tour on the SS *Venetia*, after he left the White House (*c.* 1880).

RIGHT

RIGHT
This contract ticket for a voyage in the *American Union* (1,424 tons) from London to New York was issued for eleven 'souls' of the Jones family. They were probably emigrants. The total cost was only £34. 10s. 0d.

nineteenth century. John Mason wrote to Ernst George in Lisbon saying that he wanted to sell tickets on the Lisbon-Madeira sailings of George's *Empresa Nacional* lines; he wanted sole agency in Britain and America, and would take a ten per cent commission. A week later, Ernst George replied saying, amid expressions of great pleasure in being able to do business with the admirable Mr Cook, that he accepted the offer, except for several agencies he had used in England for many years, none of them involved in the passenger business. The price of a first class ticket from Lisbon to Madeira was £5. 14s., and would Mr Cook also be interested in selling tickets on his ships to the Congo and other central African ports? This simple exchange of letters amounted to a contract.

Other agreements were more complicated. The 1888 agreement with P&O gave Cooks a sliding scale of commisions: five per cent on sales up to £50,000 in one year; six per cent on sales from £50,000 to £60,000; seven per cent on sales from £60,000 to £70,000, and so on—an indication of the amount of business Cooks hoped to do with just one company in a year.

The P&O contract also contained a clause which appeared in many Cooks' contracts. This was an agreement by Cooks to help promote the contractor's business and services by advertizing them, free of charge, in the various editions of *The Excursionist*, the *Continental Timetable* and other suitable Thomas Cook publications. Specifically with P&O, Cooks agreed to give the company more

S.S. *Pera*
BILL OF FARE.
14th Day of Sept. 1859

Mutton Broth

Roast fillet Veal
Stewed Ducks & Peas
Roast Beef
Boiled Mutton
Roast Turkey
Ham
Boiled Fowls
~~Roast~~ Mutton
Sea Pies
Roast Goose
Compot of Pigeons
Round Pork
Beefsteak Pie
Stewed Ox Tongue & Vegetables
Roast Fowls
Curry & Rice
Stewed Breast Veal & Peas

Second Course

French Tarts
Apple Charlotte
Almond Pudding
Plum Pudding
Lemon Cheese Cakes
Currant Pudding
Sandwich Pastry
Jam Puff
Stewed Quince
Jam Tartlets
Stewed Nectarines
Fancy Pastry

To this add any quantity of ~~Red~~ Sherry Madeira Claret
and Soda Water you wish & desired
also ~~any~~ amount of Spirits you please

LEFT
The passengers on SS *Pera*
did themselves well on this
menu, which apart from
offering seventeen main
courses and twelve puddings
also allowed 'any quantity' of
wines and spirits.

The depression of the 1930s reduced the amount of
high class sea travel business and so ships took on
steerage passengers who wanted to emigrate to new
countries. Steerage passengers were allowed two
pounds of meat a week and four quarts of water
daily.

The well-dressed man on a
cruise ship wore a solar topee
on shore excursions as a
symbol of imperial authority
(*c.* 1930).

TROPICAL
CRUISING
KIT

Every article of Clothing
for the Cruise can be
obtained ready for wear
at MOSS BROS.

Tropical Outfits
Sports Wear
Trunks and Suitcases
Binoculars

*Please send for a copy
of "ALL AT SEA"—
an amusing and useful
book on Cruising.*

**MOSS
BROS**
AND COMPANY LIMITED

COVENT GARDEN
Corner of King St. & Bedford St., W.C.2.
Temple Bar 4477 (10 lines).

prominence in both the Cooks' offices and their publications; Cooks would also do
their best to draw in second saloon passenger traffic as well as first saloon, and would
make a special effort to push P&O's China passenger trade.

Once the voucher system was developed, passengers could use Cook's vouchers
on board ship, just as they did in hotels, and there was usually a clause in any contract
with a shipping line covering where and how these were to be redeemed.

Though the Atlantic was the jousting ground for the big shipping companies
and for the nations they represented, it was other, smaller oceans and humbler ships
which were the setting for the early development of another major Cooks venture—
the Cook's Tour by sea.

This was something quite different. Until Cooks began to develop these tours,
people had bought tickets on ships basically to get from A to B. The Cook's Tour by
sea was a holiday on a ship: one left from A and returned to A, living on the ship, as
on a hotel, for the duration of the holiday. It was, in fact, 'cruising', though the term
did not come into general use until a quarter of a century later.

The first one took place in the seas of Scandinavia in 1875, when the Cooks developed the Midnight Sun Voyage to the North Cape with the Bergen Line. This select tour for some twenty-one passengers at a time, sailed up the coast of Norway in June on the *President Christie*, with the object of gazing on the midnight sun north of the Arctic Circle. Although it was a strange form of sun worship, it had parallels with the early morning observances of the sunrise on the mountain peaks which were a big attraction of tours in Switzerland. This first tour was a success and led to further sailing trips in Baltic waters and then in the Mediterranean.

The ships' broker with whom Cooks had made their arrangement was a Mr C. A. Gundersen who was involved in several commercial activities including herring fishing. As it happened, the year after the first Midnight Sun cruise the herring shoals diminished and business was bad so Gundersen decided to devote himself more fully to the development of the new business of ship-board holidays. In association with the Cooks, he soon had regular sailings operating in the Baltic as well as annual pilgrimages to view the Midnight Sun.

By the 1890s, the ship-board holiday business was well under way with £10 for seven-day tours on the *SS Britannia* of the Halvorsen Line and trips on the Orient Line's *Chimborazo* and *Garonne*.

By the turn of the century, the Balkans were becoming the fashionable tourist region, with Cooks advertizing cruises from Venice to Dalmatia, Bosnia and Herzegovina and places with names mostly unfamiliar to us, such as Gravosa (Dubrovnik), and Sebenic (Split).

The great era of sea-going holidays began after World War I, when an abundance of spare ships prompted lines to promote holidays at a price that would compete with land-based holidays. The Cooks devoted many pages in their publications and brochures to the new kind of Cook's Tour.

'Apart altogether from the pleasure and health giving, these cruises provide a liberal education, enabling the traveller to realize how futile it seems for the workmen of today to emulate the craftsmanship which made the Parthenon ...,' wrote an enthusiastic copywriter in *The Excursionist*.

It was plain to see to which clientele this kind of writing was addressed to: it was the middle class who were hanging on nostalgically to the values of the past in a world in which the tremors of the future were causing a fearful reaction.

In 1928, the year in which *Lady Chatterley's Lover*, *Point Counter Point*, *Anna Livia Plurabelle* and *Decline and Fall* were published, Cooks chartered the *Homeric* and *Franconia* for world cruising.

The *Homeric* was a 34,600-ton liner, the world's largest twin-screw ship; not, as Cooks pointed out, the fastest but one of the most elegant.

'The size and loftiness of the *Homeric*,' the brochure read, 'would do honour to a medieval castle.' Forward, there was a drawing room with large plate windows; behind that lay a reading room, writing room, main lounge, music room and smoking room. The main lounge was 94 feet long and had a great central dome of amber glass 'through which the sun filters as through champagne'. The dining room had 'a lofty central portion with a great inverted dome of crystal pendants reflecting in prismatic radiance the brilliancy of hundreds of concealed electric light bulbs centred on a ceiling of white and gold'.

The menu, as was traditional on liners, was enormous, so that the gymnasium, 'fitted with the latest appliances' which included an electric-ray bath and hairdressing parlours, was probably essential to the health of the passengers.

ASHORE THAT'S GOING ASH

All ashore not only climaxes the joyful anticipation of sailing. It sounds a note of caution, too: *Plan* ahead . . . see your local agent now, or Cunard White Star Line, 25 Broadway and 638 Fifth Ave., New York.

The passenger-list on the *Homeric* was an international one, gleaned from the great world-wide network of Cooks' offices, which now, as a result of the sale of the company on the retirement of Frank and Ernest Cook in 1928 had been added to the network of the famous Belgian *Compagnie des Wagons-Lits et des Grands Express Europeens.*

Many of the passengers were American, for cruising had become popular there, partly because cruises from the United States gave an opportunity to escape from the limitations of Prohibition—even gangsters enjoyed them—and partly because they satisfied the enormous American appetite for culture, which was easy to acquire through shore excursions at each port of call. Moreover, the Transatlantic run with its Blue Riband glamour enhanced by the film stars, railway barons, millionaires, artists, writers, the famous and the notorious who travelled on the ships, had helped to make all travel by ship seem glamorous—which it was.

The passengers who went on Cook's Cruises were on the whole ordinary people who would not usually have patronized the grand hotels; on a Cook's Cruise they found themselves in palatial surroundings, at a price that was not much more than that of an ordinary land holiday. In the 1925 edition of the *Travellers Gazette*, for instance, a holiday including a voyage to the Riviera, returning to England by train, was quoted at £45. 10s.

For the cruise passengers, the excitement began at the very time of boarding the ship, especially if this was at night with the liner towering like a lighted skyscraper by the quayside. At the top of the gangway the attention which was characteristic of a holiday at sea would begin when a member of the cabin staff would escort the traveller to his cabin. Almost instantly there would be a discreet knock at the door and the cabin steward would be there enquiring about preferences in pre-breakfast

Deck games satisfied the competitive instincts of cruise passengers. They included deck quoits and shuffle board (*c.* 1930).

Informal sunbathing provided an opportunity for passengers and officers to get to know each other (*c.* 1930).

refreshments, and other services required. Bath times were luxurious with fresh hot towels laid out in readiness.

The first encounter with the menu was likely to bewilder the average passenger; there were more items than in the menus of the grand hotels, while the whole day was filled with the taking of snacks and refreshments which were brought to passengers on deck as they lolled in their deck chairs or clustered round the swimming pool. In the afternoon there were bridge and whist drives, ship-board 'horse racing', competitions and the ever-available deck games. At night, dancing and theatre were on offer. The cruise ship was like a select club, or rather clubs, for there were class differences, and all those who sailed on them felt that they belonged to a special community so that if by chance they met ashore, they felt an instant kinship.

Apart from the entertainment, the real magic of the cruises lay in the experience of being at sea, a novel one for most people at that time, fulfilling the romanticism that lingered on through the 'twenties and 'thirties. There was the sea itself; the first sightings of dolphins, flying fish, Portuguese men-of-war; the heavens at night so thick with stars that travellers strolling or flirting on the top deck felt as if they were truly on a voyage in space.

During this halcyon period between the two Wars, the world of the Atlantic was ruled by two great ships, the *Queen Mary* and the *Normandie*, with the *Ile de France* playing the part of the super sophisticate — the ship that represented everything that stood for the smart world between the wars. The luxury maintained aboard most ships then seems incredible today but, like the hotels of the time, ships did not have to cope with high crew costs nor with tightly regulated working hours. The cost of fuel was low, and so were all other charges, such as port dues and maintenance.

Waving goodbye, and looking forward to the romance of a cruise.

To cruise was to belong to a cosmopolitan and sophisticated world, and shipping lines promoted the idea enthusiastically.

The swimming pool was the centre of boisterous fun as well as the place to admire the ladies.

This Donaldson Line brochure conveys the message: You won't have to lift a finger.

Moreover, shipping lines had no competition on their regular runs, for there were no transatlantic air flights, the only competition in the air was to the East and South—across landmasses where aircraft could land for refuelling—but the air fares were expensive by comparison with the ocean liners.

World War II accelerated technological advances in air transport so quickly that by 1945 the scene had totally changed. Shipping lines fought back for a time, believing that as far as leisure travel was concerned the cruise was a permanent institution.

'At last,' said a Cooks' brochure in 1949, 'you can get away from it all. Most of the regular runs are open to anyone wishing to travel for the joy of it and the sightseeing—the life aboard ship which attracted more and more holidaymakers every year until the war.'

The brochure offered nine-day cruises on an Ellerman Wilson cargo ship from Hull to Gothenburg for £28 and there was a voyage to Valparaiso, Chile, and back for £330 on the *Reina del Pacifico*. Another brochure of the time offered dreams of the future—and the end of the sea cruise. This was a Mediterranean Air Cruise, ten days by flying boat to Villefranche, from where a car would drive one to Monte Carlo, Venice and Rome for 95 guineas.

Air travel also competed with cruises across the Atlantic. A cruise to Bermuda by Holland America Line cost £200, but one could also get there by air on a seventeen-day holiday for £240, flying BOAC, British South American Airways, Pan American or Trans Canada Airlines. The flight took twenty-one hours, longer than it takes today to reach Buenos Aires, but the ship took three days and the public were no longer in the mood to believe that it is pleasanter to travel than to arrive.

The shipping companies in their mahogany and marble offices had kept aloof from the concept of popular travel but now they began to unbend. Class distinctions were abolished in the public areas of the ships, though the range of cabin prices remained; discotheques were operated alongside the ballrooms, dress became informal, and more ports of call were included in the itinerary. But the big ships were in the same situation as the big hotels; fashion had passed them by and the efforts at compromise with the new society satisfied no-one.

The glamour of the ocean had passed to the skies, which could be traversed ever more quickly in larger and larger jet aircraft that could transport people in a few hours from the prosaic realities of a British town to the exotic fantasies of tropical islands. Gradually the cruise scene faded away, only surviving in the cut-price, package tour arrangements made popular by Greek shipping lines; in sea-going motor coach tours in luxury liners around the islands of the Caribbean or Indonesia, or in marathon voyages around the world for those with the time and between £10,000 and £30,000 to spare.

Not all cruising was for fun. This party of Japanese newspapermen was travelling round South East Asia to gather information (*c.* 1930).

CHAPTER EIGHT

La Belle Epoque

In 1883, Georges Nagelmackers, a Belgian, put into operation two trains that carried sleeping cars and restaurant cars. Soon *le tout Europe* was travelling in them, including some of Thomas Cook's increasingly affluent middle-class clientele.

The first train, which left Paris on 5 June 1883, was the Orient Express, about which much has been written. It was a wonder train the like of which had never been seen in Europe. It had compartments with armchairs which converted into beds; marquetry and engraved glass panels; washing facilities; a restaurant with leather armchairs; an expert chef who could produce impeccable haute cuisine from a tiny kitchen; car attendants who looked after passenger's every whim, and it was international so that one could travel on it all the way from Paris to the Black Sea (and later to Istanbul) without having to change trains.

The Orient Express served the affluent traveller who was on his way to the East. It carried nobility, nouveau riche, industrialists, government officers, politicians— and according to legend—the most glamorous women in Europe and the most deadly spies.

It is sometimes difficult to separate fact from legend where the Orient Express is concerned and even the train itself seems to play a game of hide and seek with its own identity. Over the years it has been known as the original Orient Express (which did not at the start go to Constantinople or Stamboul, as Graham Greene calls it in his thriller about the train), the Direct Orient or Simplon Orient, the Arlberg Orient, the Tauern Orient, and has run to Athens as the Athens Express.

Whatever its name, the Orient Express remains the most renowned of all Nagelmackers' trains, though the second train that also began running in 1883, the Blue Train, almost equals its fame.

The name 'Blue Train', suggested by the colour of the carriages, came later but the train itself which ran from Paris to Rome via the French Riviera became an international symbol for the sophisticated and daring life style of those who frequented the Côte d'Azur.

Between them, the two trains summed up the new attitudes of society which, visible only at the beginning among a small international group of privileged persons, gradually spread throughout society and changed it. The Orient Express conjures up the political world of the end of the century: the world of intrigue and conspiracy which was the product of the crumbling of the established order of post-Napoleonic Europe.

In 1883, the Turkish Empire was in its final stages of collapse, despite the efforts made to bolster it up during the Crimean War, and thus Balkan Europe was in a state of turmoil which encouraged the European powers to stir up the turgid waters for their individual political motives. The stability of the Austro-Hungarian Empire which had been the European bastion against the Turks was also crumbling before

The 1938 tours to the USSR described in this brochure offered about
a dozen destinations.

OPPOSITE
Cooks teamed up with P. & O. to produce a series of tours to
India in 1936–7, and sold 3,000 in all.

Tours in India

SEASON 1936-37

IN CONJUNCTION WITH
P. & O.
STEAMERS

RIGHT
Working-class tourists were still catered for by the Cooks in
1900, as this handbill for an excursion club shows.

BELOW
The Excursionist, the newspaper which Cook had first
published in 1851, later changed its name to *The Traveller's
Gazette*. This title was thought more appropriate to the
middle-class tourists who were now Cook's main clients.

RIGHT
Working-class tourists were still catered for by the Cooks in
1900, as this handbill for an excursion club shows.

THE TRAVELLER'S GAZETTE.

*An Illustrated
Journal
Devoted to Travel*

Published Monthly
by
THOS. COOK & SON
CHIEF OFFICE
LUDGATE CIRCUS LONDON E.C.

PARIS UNIVERSAL EXHIBITION, 1900.

COOK'S

Paris Exhibition

EXCURSION CLUB.

Prospectus of Special Arrangements for

PERSONALLY CONDUCTED EXCURSIONS

TO THE

Great Paris Exhibition of 1900.

BY

Subscriptions of **1/-** per Week,

Or such other Instalments as may suit Subscribers.

OFFERING

Convenience of Easy Payments.
Choice of Various Arrangements, 2nd and 3rd
   Classes.
Economical Co-operative Rates.
Absolute Security to Depositors.
Accommodation in Paris Reserved in Advance.
Services of Guides, Interpreters, & Conductors.
Inclusive Charges.   NO EXTRAS.

THOS. COOK & SON,

Originators of the European Excursion and Tourist System.

ESTABLISHED 1841.

District Office—

61, MARKET ST., MANCHESTER.

Specially appointed by H.R.H. the Prince of Wales Passenger Agents to
the Royal British Commission for the Paris Universal Exhibition 1900,
   Vienna 1873, Philadelphia 1876, Paris 1878, Colonial and Indian 1886,
   Chicago 1893; also specially appointed Agents for the Antwerp Exhibition
   1894, Amsterdam 1895, Brussels 1897, and Stockholm 1897; also sole
   Passenger Agents for the Vienna Jubilee Exhibition, 1898, for
   England, France, and the United States of America.

(216:99.)

the growing strength of Prussian Germany. Britain and France were concerned
about the European balance of power but their attention and their forces were
involved in their colonial wars. All the powers were wary too of the Russian interest
in Turkey, Afghanistan and Persia.

In this volatile situation the Orient Express which ran through Europe to
Constantinople and was the highway to the Eastern Mediterranean, Egypt and the
Far East, was a ready made location, at least as far as the inventive and imaginative
minds were concerned, for the intrigues that were supposed to be taking place in the
European chess game.

The Blue Train reflected another aspect of society, for it was a meeting place for
the leisured rich, the class of person who had money and wealth by birth, like sons of
the landed gentry and of the commercial nouveau riche of Britain and the idle

Special working-class groups were handled by the Cooks but the profit for the company lay in providing travel for the middle classes (1910).

nobility of the Russian court. These people, like the courtiers of Louis XIV's age, were at a loss to know what to do with their time. Their class of society did not work, unless they were eccentrics like Tolstoy, and they therefore had to find other things to do; it was for them that a seasonal social round was invented. Travel for such people was no longer in pursuit of learning and self improvement but simply for pleasure. John Mason Cook, though not naturally inclined to approve of idleness, nevertheless recognized that here was a new class of clientele for the Cook's Tour system and, while continuing his cheap excursions and tourist systems, his seaside cheap tickets and his conducted tours to Europe, he began to fall in with the new trend of a public that could afford his more expensive overseas tours.

'We have watched,' he wrote in 1882, a year before the Orient Express, 'the growth of pleasure travel as none others have had the opportunity to do; and from a

recent investigation we find that for every one person who travelled for pleasure fifty years ago one thousand travelled in 1882.' He then goes on to talk about the advantages of the Cook's Tour system and asks, 'Why is the system so popular? Because those who are fortunate enough to have nothing to do but enjoy life find in it boundless resources of pleasure.'

Thus was born a totally new attitude to travel, an attitude which accorded well with a new attitude to life; the *Belle Epoque*, with its sense of fun and gaiety and its *joie de vivre*, broke through the formal life-style of earlier years.

Paris was the capital of this new style in living, and the hundreds who had visited her in the first years of Cook's Tours grew into millions. For £2.18s.od one could travel first class to the Ville Lumière, while third class cost only £1.2s.9d. Hotel

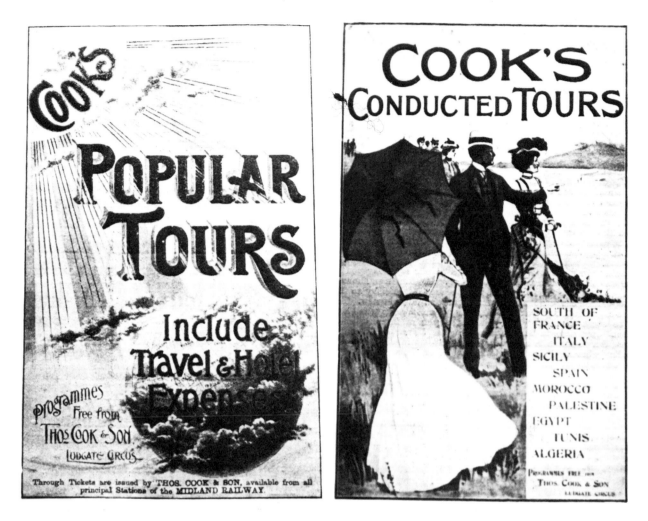

coupons were offered by the Cooks for 12s. in Britain, 12s. 6d. in the US and 8s. or 8s. 9d. in Europe; they provided bed, two or three meals and lights.

Dorothy Menpes and her artist husband Mortimer, produced a book about Paris in the Edwardian period. She described the city's atmosphere, to which its boulevards contributed much: 'boulevards *des affaires*, boulevards of fashion, boulevards for the rich, boulevards for the poor, boulevards of every kind.' She also wrote about the *ateliers*, or workrooms, where the poor slaved for long hours making the latest creations of Paris fashion; the student quarter; the Latin Quarter where 'everywhere one hears the clattering of glasses and the shouting of the "garçons". This is the real Bohemia. The streets are filled with noisy, rollicking students, singing and dancing, generally arm in arm with some brilliant gay lady dressed in the height of fashion.'

Montmartre Dorothy Menpes described as 'a scene of all that is wild, mad and extravagant. Nothing is too terrible, too eccentric for the Montmartrois mind.' This was the quarter where the artists and writers lived and where modern art was being created by the Impressionists and by the young Picasso, Braque, Matisse and others who frequented the cafes and cabarets that Dorothy Menpes describes.

ABOVE
Conducted tours were led by an experienced guide who served his clients in the same way as the private courier had done for the leisured classes of former years (*c*. 1900).

ABOVE LEFT
Cook's popular tours were designed for the growing class of lower-middle-class customers and were a no-frills version of the regular tours (1903).

Cook's tours included
transfers from stations to
hotels in taxis like this
(*c.* 1900).

Cook's tours included
transfers from stations to
hotels in taxis like this
(*c.* 1900).

Most city tours before World
War I were arranged by
horse-drawn carriage like this
one in Cologne (*c.* 1900).

'There are cabarets of Heaven, Hell and Death,' she wrote, 'where the waiters are dressed respectively as angels and undertakers. You enter the cabaret through the Golden Gates, the angel Gabriel guards the entrance—an angel with an ill-shaven face, surrounded by a long flaxen wig and a halo. When you call for a drink the ferocious angel at your elbow growls "Thy will be done".'

In another cabaret, Le Neant, coffins were used as tables and the walls were decorated with skulls and bones. Drinks were described as draughts promoting cholera or cancer, and the master of ceremonies entertained his customers with lectures on death and decay.

Clearly, Paris offered a freedom and excitement that both shocked and fascinated the average Cooks tourist, and one can imagine the thrills of horror and repugnance felt by those daring enough to visit such entertainments.

The company certainly did not 'recommend' these places but felt it their duty to visit them so that they might warn their customers, who were no doubt thus encouraged to join the night excursions on offer (not from Cooks, who did not operate night tours until the post-war years). These took tourists to homosexual bars, prostitutes' haunts, and apache bars, usually ending up with a flourish at the Moulin Rouge.

After Paris, the most shocking and therefore the most fascinating place in Europe at which to spend a holiday before World War I was Monte Carlo. Gambling establishments were not new to Europe for they had existed at such spas as Baden-Baden and Wiesbaden for years but under a discreet cloak of privacy and, besides, they were patronized only by the rich and noble. The shocking thing about Monte Carlo was that it was designed to attract those who had the money to go there.

Having sold many of the lands of Monaco, including, in 1861, the resort of Menton, to Napoleon III on his takeover of formerly Italian territory, Prince Charles of Monaco was still on the verge of bankruptcy when he had the brilliant idea of calling in Monsieur Francois Blanc who had recently turned both Baden-Baden and Bad Homburg into profitable spas. The prince came to an arrangement whereby Monsieur Blanc could have the exclusive gambling rights in Monaco in return for a royalty on his earnings. Within a year of the opening of the Casino, Prince Charles was making so much money that he abolished taxation in his principality. Monte Carlo's success did not go down well in neighbouring Nice, the leading resort on the Côte d'Azur before Monte Carlo's casino was opened. A campaign of defamation was begun, well supported by those who saw in the new trends nothing but a modern Sodom and Gomorrah, and by the Italians who had felt cheated at annexation of part of their former coastline.

Like most scandals, that surrounding Monte Carlo profited the vilified because of the publicity it aroused, and the casino business grew apace. Nagelmackers, taking advantage of the increased traffic on his Blue Train, launched into hotel building, and Cooks began to describe in glowing terms in their *Travellers Gazette*, the attractions of both Nice and Monte Carlo.

During this whole pre-World War I period, no-one would have dreamt of going to the Côte d'Azur in summer, a custom which came later with the Americans in the period between the wars. The high point of the *Belle Epoque* season was spring and carnival time, and Cooks developed an itinerary for this period, which began with an arrival in Nice on the same day that King Carnival appeared, to the accompaniment of bands, artillery salutes, illuminations by electric light and festivities at the Nice casino, which did not include gambling.

The following day the Cooks' tourists would watch the procession of the Masqueraders and a Twilight procession, followed by a day and night charitable Fête at the Casino. Then came the great day of the Battle of Flowers and Gala Procession. But even this was not the end, for three more days of Masked Balls and Grand Carnival Processions were to follow before a gigantic firework display brought the week's festivities to a close.

It was all a stupendous £4. 1s. 6d. worth to those who took the Carnival cheap return fare offered by Cooks.

As far as Monte Carlo was concerned, Cooks trod cautiously, remembering the majority of their tourists who were still plodding earnestly through the ruins of Pompeii and across the deserts of the Holy Land intent on combining learning with pleasure on their holiday. When Cooks' brochures did describe the Casino they claimed that their only purpose was to inform, not to encourage.

'The great attraction of Monte Carlo,' the Cooks' *Handbook to Health Resorts* said, 'is the Casino where the gambling tables are open from 11 am to 11 pm and even later in the club.'

Two Cook's brochure covers.

Winter Sunshine

SEE SPECIAL ANNOUNCEMENT
ON PAGE 38

1949 - 1950

COOK'S WORLD TRAVEL SERVICE

Solid rubber-tyred charabancs
with no protection against the
weather but able to cope with
larger numbers than horse
carriages were used by the
Cooks for cheaper tours in the
larger cities (c. 1905).

Deauville, one of the
fashionable watering places in
north-west France, had the
charisma of class and wealth
that British south coast
resorts could not emulate.

The pier at Nice, more
magnificent than any of its
British counterparts, was
subsequently damaged in a
storm and had to be pulled
down.

Pointing out that the respectable inhabitants of Monaco, Nice and Menton were in favour of closing down the Casino, the *Handbook* added that it made a profit of some £2,000,000 a year and benefited the citizens of Monaco. The *Handbook* then launched into a detailed description of the sumptuous rooms of the Casino, which were designed by Garnier, the architect of the Paris Opera House, and of the method of play in roulette and trente et quatre. 'Women,' the Handbook says, 'are there in numbers, fierce and eager as they grasp their winnings (and sometimes those of others).'

Despite Queen Victoria's disapproval and the hesitation of the Bishop of Gibraltar in allowing the building of a church in Monaco, the principality flourished and the tourists flocked in 'to have a look', inevitably ending up by having a flutter.

The demand for luxury, pleasure and excitement during the *Belle Epoque* was limited on the whole to those who had the money and the leisure and the inclination for a life of hedonist pleasure. Their views and attitudes were well expressed by Edward VII, a frequent visitor to Paris and the Côte d'Azur, who, according to Hector Bolitho writing in the *Evening News* in 1937, on being asked whether he would care to visit the ruins at Luxor exclaimed, 'Why should we go and see the tumble-down Temple? When we get there, nothing to be seen, like going to Rome to see the theatre of somebody and only two stones left.' The view of the King and other members of high bourgeoisie which he represented was not shared however by others who took Cook's Tours to all the, by now, familiar cultural places and to the endless exhibitions organized by the great cities of Europe.

To satisfy this growing demand for travel, the Cooks negotiated with all the steamship and railway lines operating not only in the fashionable regions but in many to which only the more esoteric customer would travel.

In the United States (which had grown in 1889 and 1890 by the admission of the states of North and South Dakota, Montana, Washington, Idaho and Wyoming into the Union and was profiting by its unity), Cook found a growing market for sea travel and hastened to charter ships for this operation.

In 1892 John Mason made a contract with the North Atlantic Steamship Company of Boston for cruises to the West Indies on the steamship *Britannia*. Like most of his steamship contracts, this one put the financial and operational responsibility on the steamship company, and Cooks was limited to printed matter, canvassing for business and 'other matters'.

It says a good deal for the name of the company at this period that the steamship line was eager enough to be adopted by the Cooks to pay for $1,500-worth of the advertising campaign and to allow the Cooks to hold the moneys obtained from passengers until the ship sailed. The commission for Cooks' sales was ten per cent.

At the same time, Cooks were extending their business over the American railroad network, getting sales concessions for travel over the whole country. The company was also able to put its own world-wide business at the disposal of the American railroads. An agreement with the Pennsylvania Railroad Company in 1893 covered the arrangement and distribution of the railroad's 'printed and ornamental matter' in Europe through Cooks' offices. The railroad would pay a fee of £100 per annum for each office in which their material appeared, and chose initially to use the Paris, Cologne, Vienna and Florence offices. An agreement with the New York Central Lines gave the shipping company a full page advertisement in each issue of the Cooks' monthly publications, *The American Travelers' Gazette* and the *Ocean Sailing List*.

ABOVE
The Casino in Monte Carlo was
built by Garnier, who also built
the Paris Opera, and its imposing
facade gave a certain 'tone' to the
business of gambling.

TOP
Promenading, as here in Monte
Carlo, was a popular pastime at
resorts and it gave everyone an
opportunity both to show off and
to criticise others.

Cook's arranged many of
Edward VII's little
continental sorties. Here the
King is talking to a Cook's
representative prior to
boarding the funicular to the
top of Vesuvius.

Cook also introduced himself into the market of rich and influential customers and it was no doubt for their benefit that he listed at the back of his Nile brochures the royal families which were his customers in Europe. For rich Americans, he organized private tours to Egypt, including voyages up the Nile in dahabeahs, or private steamers, where passengers were treated like royalty. One of the contracts made at this period states that Cook is chartering the steamer *SS Lyderhorn* of the Hardanger company for a three-week cruise by Baron Rothschild and this, too, must have impressed the rising American millionaire class.

The wealthy cream of Cooks' clientele were demanding, and the company had continually to improve its services to satisfy their requirements. Cooks' men multiplied at every port, station and resort and so did the Cooks' offices.

The Nile steamers, which were the jewels of the Cooks' crown, were supplied with every possible amenity, including free medical services. In the contract Cooks made with the doctors on the Nile steamers, it was stipulated that the doctor should be entertaining to passengers but that he should not 'take part in any way in the management or working of the ship, but should he hear of any complaint or suggestions from passengers he is kindly to report the same to the manager of the steamer for his attention.'

By this time, there was an army of people working for Cooks all over the world, and the doctors were only one of the many who served the Cooks' customers. The key jobs in the Cooks' empire were the agents or local managers, and they, too, were obliged to observe strict contractual rules laid down by John Mason Cook.

A certain Albert Edward Metcalfe, who joined Cooks in 1892, was told he could not himself decide on the use of the company's funds for any purpose whatsoever, and was given a salary of £120. Before he was given the job, however, he was asked to put up a fidelity guarantee of £1,500. There must have been considerable opportunities for making good money in the Cooks' service, for in addition to salary there was a range of commissions available to the agents: half a per cent for commissionable tickets and a quarter per cent for those that were not; a one per cent commission for hotel coupon sales; a ten per cent commission for the sale of guide books; and a ten per cent commission for profits made on the banking business.

A main area of traffic was still across Europe to the Middle East and East, and once conditions in the Balkans began to favour the establishment of railways, the

Cooks arrived, contracts in hand, to tie up their arrangements with the Balkan and Austrian railways. 1892 was a successful year, with the Austrian State Railways, Hungarian State Railways, the Emperor Ferdinand's Northern Railway and the Bosnia and Herzegovina Railway all signing on the dotted line and giving Cooks five-and-a-half per cent commission on every ticket sold. The terms of business were astonishingly relaxed, with the Cooks having to present a record of the sales made on behalf of the railways only once a year.

Other companies were not quite so accommodating. The contract with the Mediterranean Railway of Italy demanded payment in gold for the tickets which Cooks sold. Evidently, the exchange rate for gold went against the company, for the Cooks complained about the damage caused by the increasing rate of exchange. Eventually, wanting to accommodate their chief retailer of tickets, the Mediterranean Railway allowed the Cooks to pay for tickets issued in Italy in notes of the Banca Nazionale instead of gold.

In Australia, too, the Cooks found that negotiating was a tougher business. The Victorian Railways Commission allowed the company to sell their tickets in Europe, Asia, Africa and America but demanded payment in full, monthly and with a guarantee of £2,000. Only then were the Cooks paid their commission of ten per cent.

In these years of the *Belle Epoque*, the members of the Cook family were all busily travelling around the world in search of new arrangements with the world's

The funicular cars, named Vesuvius and Etna, suffered at the hands of local saboteurs who saw in them a threat to their business of carrying passengers to the summit of the volcano in sedan chairs. J. M. Cook threatened to stop tourism to Vesuvius if the sabotage continued, and won the day (*c.* 1890).

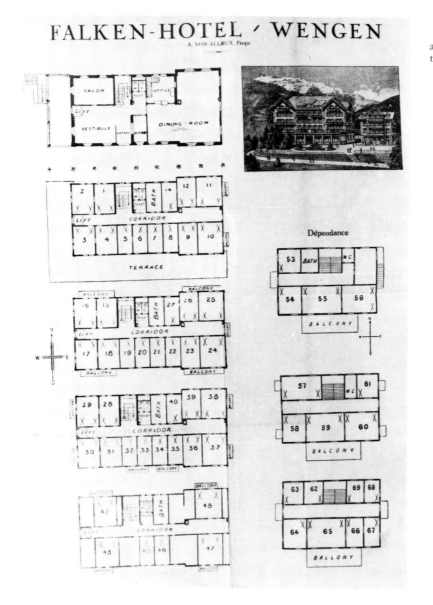

FALKEN-HOTEL / WENGEN
A. VON ALLMEN, Propr.

Thousands of hotels had contracts with the Cooks and many of these provided the company with bedroom plans, the customer even choosing his own room.

transport systems and hotels. Father, son and grandchildren were the tough professional nucleus of the business and few things escaped their eagle eyes: from the fact that the manager in Cairo was ordering Yardleys soap instead of the one recommended by John Mason, to the discovery of a discrepancy in the accounts in America.

As they consolidated and expanded their vast business, the Cooks were aware that a tide of change was taking place in the world and in their business, but the two leaders of the team, Thomas and John Mason Cook died before the century turned. It was now up to the grandsons Frank, Ernest and Thomas to take the business forward into an era where the car, the charabanc and the aeroplane would revolutionize travel, and the wireless and telephone would provide a means of controlling the ever-growing network that they had inherited.

Scandinavia, one of the first
cruise destinations for Cooks,
continued to have its own
brochure well into the 1950s.

The 'Great West' included Alaska in this 1950s brochure.

CHAPTER NINE

The Family Business

The astonishing growth of the Cook's Tour business, especially in the 1880s and 1890s, was helped by the fact that it was a family business. That there were few competitors in the early years indicates there was little profit to attract other entrepreneurs and, in fact, Cook's only contemporary rival, Henry Gaze, also ran his business with the help of his son.

As a family business, overheads could be kept to a minimum and hours stretched to a maximum without fear of complaints or slacking. Right from the beginning of his marriage, Thomas Cook made sure that every member of his family contributed to its finances. Soon after marrying Marianne, Cook had set up a temperance boarding house in Leicester, and it was his wife who ran it. Marianne must have been a woman of character. It was she who, having been persuaded to teetotalism by an advocate of the cause known as the Birmingham Blacksmith, convinced her husband that there could be no half measures where the demon drink was concerned. So it was that Thomas had to pour away gallons of beer that he kept in the cellar of his house. He did draw the line at wasting his best beer, though, and he sent this to his brother-in-law, commenting afterwards that the barrel must have been tapped on its journey as it did not arrive full.

As a first step to moving his business to London, Cook set up another boarding house there, in Great Russell Street, opposite the British Museum. Once again, it was Marianne Cook who ran the place, with Cook using its conservatory as his office. It was here that he was interviewed by Edmund Yates, one of Charles Dickens' reporters on a magazine called *All the World Over*.

By the time Cook moved into Fleet Street he had been in the excursions and tourist business for twenty years and his son John Mason, some fourteen years. John Mason's earliest recollection of assisting his father was of helping to lead Midlands working people on to the trains on which Thomas Cook was transporting them to London for the Great Exhibition of 1851. As a young man of sixteen, John Mason travelled up and down on these exhibition trains, more often than not having to sleep on them as they shuttled back and forth from Leicester, Nottingham and other Midland towns to London. He also helped in the printing business, often staying up all hours of the night packing and distributing the temperance publications that his father printed.

After such a hard apprenticeship it is not surprising that John Mason wanted to get away from his father: it may be that it was during these years that the two men discovered that they irritated each other. Very likely this was because they were both autocratic and liked to have their own way as much as because of their business disagreements. Matters came to a head when John Mason joined his father at the Fleet Street office. By this time John Mason was a married man with three children, Frank, Ernest and Thomas, and he wanted to run things his own way. He had also

Thomas Cook at the height of his fame in the 1880s. After this his son John Mason took over the business.

Mrs Marianne Cook, a strict
teetotaller and capable
businesswoman, who ran the
Cook hotels and boarding
houses until the 1870s.

half come to the conclusion that though his father might be a pioneer of travel, as a
businessman he was too altruistic and erratic ever to be really successful.

The fact was that by the 1870s the nature of the business had changed
considerably and the amateur enthusiasm of Thomas Cook's early excursions and
tours was not enough to keep it growing and solvent. With every year that passed,
John Mason's irritation increased, no doubt causing much anguish in the family
circle, which included his sister Annie who also worked in Fleet Street.

As the business grew, so did the pressure on John Mason who did not yet have
the support of his own sons, who were at boarding school. So the friction between
the Cook men worsened. One of the main areas of contention was the quarrel
between John Mason and the American partner, Jenkins.

Thomas bought property in Jerusalem against John Mason's wishes, he sided
with Jenkins, and on returning from his first excursion round the world to find that
John Mason had paid off the debts that had accrued as a result of moving into bigger
premises at Ludgate Circus, he accused him of robbing him to raise the money.
There is no doubt that Thomas was put out, as well he might have been, for he had
worked like a demon to keep his business afloat for over twenty-five years, and here
was his son telling him that he had made enough money in two or three years to pay
off their debts.

There is no direct evidence of what Thomas Cook's wife and daughter Annie felt
about this bitter quarrel but it seems that they sided with their father. Outraged by
their ingratitude for all the things he had achieved for the family, John Mason
penned a document in which he laid out all the alleged complaints against him by his
family, and his answers to them. In it he points out that as he had paid off the debts
on the hotel, in which his mother and sister lived rent and food free, they could
hardly say he did not care for the family. He also refers to an offer of £1,000 per
annum made to his father on condition that he retire from the business.

John Mason Cook, a
formidable character who
built the excursion and tourist
business into a travel empire.

The holograph document still in existence in the Thomas Cook archives has a
slightly distraught ring to it which does not accord totally with the image one has of
the head of a growing worldwide business. But he evidently was able to keep the
various sections of his life separate for while he was quarrelling with his father he
also kept a cool eye on the business and on his competitors, about whom he wrote to
J. E. Mitchell, the man in charge of arrangements for the Centennial Exhibition in
the City of Philadelphia:

'We are the only people in Europe that can carry out such arrangements [to run
tours to the exhibition]. Our only imitator can only issue the Railway companies'
tickets at the *same* fare as they can be obtained from the Railways.'

By 1878 John Mason's nerves were beginning to fray. He was virtually running
the business single-handed, making the contracts, keeping an eye on his overseas
offices, ensuring that his tourists were well-looked after, and coping with the
increasing demand for Cook's Tours and tickets at the Ludgate Circus office as well
as developing such new systems as the Circular Coupon (the forerunner of the
travellers cheque, first issued in New York in 1873), and launching a railway
timetable.

Rightly or wrongly, feeling rejected and ill-treated by his family, he issued an
ultimatum to his father.

'I will not sign or enter into any new arrangements for partnership with you
upon any terms.' What he was saying was that either his father left him in sole charge
of the business or he would get out.

Thomas Cook did not have much choice. He was now seventy and although he
did not want to admit it, he knew his son was the better businessman.

Meanwhile John Mason was writing to a friend in America:

The worst feature of the matter is that my father will not assist me in prosecuting
Jenkins but on the contrary wants me to sell my share and interest in the

Annie Cook, daughter. Her love affair with one of the office clerks was brought to an end by her brother. She died accidentally in her bath.

goodwill of our name and connection either to himself or as a joint stock Company. So that I may be paid my share of the amount we have been robbed of and Jenkins may be reinstated with the power to use the name of Cooks and Cook's Tours.

No doubt Marianne and Annie both tried their best to stop the quarrel. Annie wrote to her brother, but his reply was uncompromising!

It is quite natural for you to believe your father and I do not want to say one word more to alter your views. You asked me to come to Russell Street, to go through the boarding house accounts with my father. This I cannot feel justified in doing.

It was in November of the same year, 1878, that John Mason confronted Jenkins, accusing him of fraud and embezzlement. Jenkins sued John Mason for damages of 50,000 dollars. The case dragged on with Jenkins avoiding an appearance in court and then offering to end the litigation. John Mason, acting true to his character, refused to give up. When his manager in New York, a man called Faulkner, wired him to say that Jenkins was ill and that according to his doctors only an end to the litigation could save his life John Mason wired back, 'Yes with judgement in our favour'.

By now, John Mason's sons were old enough to enter the business and their father could at last rely on their support to share the heavy burden of trying to control a world-wide Empire of travel at a time when the only means of communication were by mail and telegraph, costly items, and when it took weeks to get to any of the offices that required the firm hand of their master.

The size of the business kept all the men busy and the correspondence, all handwritten and copied by the holograph system (by which the ink was transferred to a flimsy sheet under the original), flew fast and furious.

Frank Cook (right), the eldest son of John Mason, inherited some of his father's business flair. His brother Thomas, known as Bert (left), left the business when his father died and after sowing some wild oats became a Norfolk farmer. Here they are seen in Greek dress.

'Last year's account,' writes John Mason to his trusted manager Faulkner, who had now moved to Cairo, 'have been thrown back a considerable time thro' discrepancies in the balancing . . . it is absolutely necessary there should be someone you can rely upon representing your department both at Assiout and Assuan.'

But finding reliable staff was not easy, nor was keeping control of what they were doing or getting straight answers to his queries.

'Neither your letter nor Mr Spiller,' he complains to Faulkner a little later, 'give me the information I want . . . I wanted a clear and distinct statement . . . I do not mean that I want a rambling letter such as the enclosed . . .'

After his experience with Jenkins, John Mason was on the alert for any signs of dishonesty. He would not allow his staff to speculate with the company's money and took Faulkner to task for buying some American railway bonds and, at another time, Turkish bonds.

Having settled his domestic problems with his father he now found himself with another. This time it concerned his sister Annie who had fallen in love with one of John Mason's clerks, called Higgins. John Mason made his attitude crystal clear; either the courtship ended or Higgins would find himself without a job and his sister cut out of her interest in the company. Writing to his New York manager, John Mason explained the situation.

I told them both at once that I could not have a brother-in-law member of the staff and if they were married he would have to leave our service. He appealed to me in various ways but I declined to move from my decisions. He has left the service and I know no more than you do when the marriage is to take place.

The marriage never did take place for Annie was found dead in her bath on Sunday November 8, 1880. The inquest verdict was accidental death through drowning and it was suggested that this was due to being overcome by fumes from the geyser which heated the bath water.

The Grand Tour idea has persisted until the present day, though more in the form of a marathon coach tour. This brochure was published in about 1950.

Travel is sometimes said to be a kind of play-acting, so perhaps it is not altogether surprising to see John Mason Cook re-enacting the death of Gordon.

ABOVE RIGHT
Ernest (seated) and Thomas (Bert) Cook. Ernest later built up the foreign money side of the business and when he retired devoted his own inheritance to buying properties, including Montacute and the Bath Assembly Rooms, which he later presented to the nation.

John Mason's aggressive behaviour and touchiness continued throughout his later years and one receives the impression of a man almost overwhelmed by the burden of the business and hitting out at every imagined slight or sign of weakness in his organization. His correspondence is full of such incidents.

He is angry about the muddle over a stop-over at Singapore on the Cook's World Cruise and complains that his son Frank who has gone out to superintend the cruise has been misinformed. 'I shall want a full explanation,' he says, using one of his favourite phrases.

He had time to upbraid a hotelier in Damascus: 'I am very much surprised to find that you are still adopting the system of writing and talking against me ...' He complains to the Minister of Antiquities in Cairo about the state of the temples in Karnak: 'there have been several complaints ... [that] your guardians at Karnak themselves disfigure the hieroglyphics and points of interest at the ruins.'

He also started a long feud with a Dr Mattson, an American traveller whom he refused to take on an Egypt trip because the doctor was travelling with a young lady who was evidently not his wife. Dr Mattson, according to John Mason, turned on him in a 'demonic manner' and on his return to America published a pamphlet warning the American people not to travel on Cooks Tours.

While all this was going on John Mason kept up a steady stream of instructions to his sons, sometimes taking one or other of them on his trips and at other times leaving them in charge at one point or another of the chain of offices that ringed the world.

In contrast to the fire and brimstone of John Mason's business letters, there are a vast number of letters written personally to people seeking his charity. One Leicester person writes, 'It so happens that I have just £2 cash for a trip somewhere and ask if it would be possible for you to get me a railway pass;' and receives the pass. In the Thomas Cook archives there are scores of letters thanking him for help of one kind or another, including among them the British and Foreign Sailors' Society, the Band of Hope, the English Lake District Association, the British Opthalmic Hospital in Jerusalem, the Cab Drivers' Benevolent Association, and many others. He was not always an easy touch, however; when the widow Odescalchi, who had been married to one of his Egyptian staff, wrote to ask for money and a free Nile pass, he told her he considered he had given her enough and that he would send her a pass but it would only be valid for trips to visit her husband's grave.

As we have seen, by the 1890s everyone of note travelled with the Cooks, from the Czar of Russia and the British Royal family downwards, and John Mason looked after his distinguished clients with extra zeal. To the wife of the painter Watts he sent a bottle of lotion for her husband's eczema, and he was assiduous in attending to the travel needs of the Duchess of Rutland who wrote personally to him explaining how busy she was, in reply presumably, to a request from John Mason that she should attend some function. 'The 25th is the Queen's birthday and I have engagements to fulfill . . .,' writes the Duchess. 'I am sure I can't be wanted for more than an hour or an hour and a half. It would fatigue me *unnecessarily* and it is only by being very careful in the *Management* of my time that I can be present at the numerous places where little duties have to be done.' Tiresome though they might sometimes have been, the rich and powerful were of value to Cook's Tours and their names were often listed at the back of guides to the Nile steamer trips.

Aware that their patronage recommended Cook's Tours to others lower down on the social scale, John Mason was constantly on the alert for opportunities to serve the great and the famous.

On reading in the newspaper that the Duke of Connaught was planning to return from India he wrote,

'Seeing in the paper that your Royal Highness is contemplating returning from India via Japan, China, America etc to England I hope you will pardon the liberty I am taking in offering the services of my firm . . .'

There was not a single aspect of the business that escaped John Mason's attention. He had virtually sacrificed his life to it and the worldwide growth of the Cook's Tours system at the end of the nineteenth century was undoubtedly due to his singlemindedness. He had a secret desire to have his work recognized, and when the company's Jubilee banquet was arranged in 1891 he commissioned a writer called Fraser Rae to tell the story of the Cook's Tours in a book entitled *The Business of Travel*.

What would have pleased him more than anything would have been some public recognition for his work especially as he felt, quite rightly, that the Cook's Tour system had served the Empire well in Egypt and in India. It was not to be, though, ironically, he and his son Frank were decorated by the German Emperor for their services in arranging a tour to the Holy Land.

After the 1880s John Mason's sons were drawn more and more into the business and one can detect the strong influence of their father in their style of management.

Frank, who was the elder son, was as meticulous as John Mason about instructions being obeyed to the letter and, like his father, was constantly coming across the frailties of his staff and suppliers. He wrote to Thomas (called Bert in the family) in London telling him that the flags that Edgington had sent them for the Nile steamers had been specified as $3\frac{1}{2}$ by $2\frac{1}{2}$ yards but were actually only $3\frac{1}{2}$ by $2\frac{1}{4}$

Another costume piece: this time it is Frank Cook on an Egyptian donkey used to carry tourists to the pyramids.

yards. He complained, too, about the quality of the glasses supplied by Green & Nephew which he said 'are simply disgraceful. They look like pothouse tumblers.' The cork mats for the bathrooms of the Nile steamers were never the same two seasons running, a washing machine arrived with a broken side, and the worst muddle of all was with the order for biscuits, which had been over-supplied. Wafers, gingers, oaten, water and Albert had arrived in such vast quantities that 'I don't know what we are going to do with them'. Moreover, Frank adds, 'Huntley and Palmer must have sent us some old stock at any rate of breakfast and toast biscuits, as Lord Waterford complained so strongly about them that we had to purchase some others.'

Thomas Cook died in 1892 and John Mason followed him eight years later, so by the turn of the century the two men who had built up the world's first and largest tourist system were dead. They had between them started a tourist movement among British people which the whole world has followed.

Thomas Cook dreamt of railways for the million but he could hardly have imagined flights for the hundreds of million who use the airways today. Even his grandsons Frank, Ernest and Thomas, who carried on the family business in much the same style as their father, had no inkling in their lifetime of the gigantic changes to take place in the post-war years.

By this time they were no longer associated with the business of Cook's Tours, for they had retired in 1928, selling the business to the *Cie des Wagons-Lits et des grands Express Europeens* of Belgium in whose hands it remained until World War II, when the German occupation of Brussels and Paris caused it to pass into the charge of the Custodian of Enemy Property. Owing to the world-wide ramifications of the Cook Empire, the British government arranged for the company to be bought by several British railway companies, as a result of which Cooks became state-owned when the railways were nationalized in 1948. The subsequent history is told in the final chapter.

CHAPTER TEN

Between the Wars

The Cook's Tour between the wars reflects the uncertainties of a society in which an old way of life is crossing a watershed into a new one which can be only dimly perceived. As in most transitional states, there is an overlap between past and future with nuclei of reaction and counteraction as focal points for the warring forces. In politics these conflicting forces crystallized into extreme left and right wing ideologies; in art into the academic versus the avant-garde factions; and in leisure into the Baedeker tourists and the hedonists.

Although eighty years had elapsed since the first Cook's Tour, a landmark in the popularization of travel, in 1921 only 700,000 British people travelled abroad. There is no record to show exactly how many of these were leisure travellers but if one considers that a large number of Britons were travelling abroad in the service of the Empire and Empire trade, the likelihood is that there were few tourists indeed, and, in fact, it is evident from the Cooks' strategies during the *Belle Epoque* that those who did go abroad were either the rich or the new middle classes.

Of tourists from other nations there were few: some Americans, some Germans, a few from the colonies. The British were the pioneers of tourism and in the period between the wars they still led the way.

In the years immediately after World War I, when a country fit for heroes to live in still seemed a reasonable objective, demands for regular annual holidays grew. In 1919 at the first International Labour Conference in Sweden it was suggested that the subject be put on the agenda for the next meeting. In Britain in 1925, a Bill for holidays with pay was blocked in the house of Commons. In 1936 the International Labour Organization at last brought the subject up, but the British government delegates abstained from voting. Considering that the British were leaders in the idea of cheap holidays and foreign travel, and had even instituted the Bank Holiday in 1871, this hardly helped to develop the holiday market between the wars.

Nevertheless, by the end of the period there were some 1.4 million British people travelling abroad each year, either on business or for pleasure. Many of these travelled on the Cook's Tour system and on excursions promoted by men like Sir Henry Lunn, and the youth movement organizations such as the Co-operative Holidays Association, Workers Travel Association, and the Polytechnic Touring Association, all of which encouraged and arranged tours abroad for young people. Their objectives were the traditional ones which had inspired Thomas Cook in his early days, and which were defined by the Trades Union Congress when they promoted the idea of regular annual holidays 'for the freely chosen development of the human personality'. This concept of the holiday was already going out of fashion when it was propounded, for holidays had begun to become a search for pleasure only and not for enlightenment.

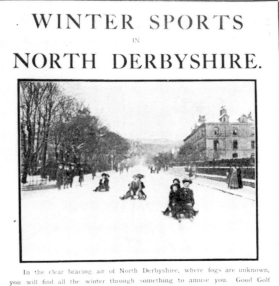

WINTER SPORTS
IN
NORTH DERBYSHIRE.

In the clear bracing air of North Derbyshire, where fogs are unknown, you will find all the winter through something to amuse you. Good Golf and Motoring, or Hunting with the High Peak Lovers of high-class music will appreciate the Pavilion Concerts in the evening, and theatre-goers will find good companies playing at the new Opera House.

To those who like Switzerland, BUXTON in snow is specially attractive. They understand winter sports there, and ski-ing, curling, sleighing and skating get into full swing directly the winter comes.

TRY A WEEK-END AT BUXTON.

Winter Sports
Season 1923-4
THOS. COOK & SON.

ABOVE
Keeping the holiday spirit alive during wartime. Cook's offered summer holidays on the English Riviera and winter holidays in Britain's answer to Switzerland— Buxton.

ABOVE RIGHT
After World War I winter sports were promoted successfully as a more sophisticated form of leisure than the more mundane summer holiday.

The pleasure principle in British holidays had already been established with the coming of cheap fares and the development of the seaside. Here attempts to justify a holiday on health reasons were soon forgotten in the hurly burly of entertainment, social freedom and sexual liberty that the popular resorts provided.

After World War I the masses in Britain took to the seaside in increasing numbers and the resorts provided them with all the fun of the fair. Blackpool received seven million visitors a year (Cooks charged £7. 14s. 9d. from London with hotel for one week), Southend five and a half, Brighton, Margate, Ramsgate, Hastings, Bournemouth and Southport all had between one and three million, and new resorts were setting themselves up in competition with rival attractions. Good amenities and entertainments were the keynotes, with Blackpool spending £1.5 million to extend its promenade and £250,000 on improving the Winter Garden. Hastings spent nearly £300,000 on its promenade and Pavilion. The seaside industry thrived.

The few who went abroad, though no longer confined to the leisure classes of the *Belle Epoque*, looked on themselves as a cut above the common mass of holiday-makers in Britain. Most of them felt an obligation to be interested in the countries they visited, and the authors of the period supplied their reading requirements with books written during their travels and as fillers between more serious work. Their travel books created a *genre* with which those who liked to think of themselves as cultured travellers could identify, and some still do. It set them apart and therefore

By the 1930s winter sports resorts had sprung up all over Europe and the development of such mechanical aids as ski hoists, chair lifts and cable cars was making skiing an effortless sport.

above their fellow tourists, a characteristic which is only human but which finds in travels, as in gastronomy and oenology, a particularly productive soil.

Although some of these writers, like Lawrence, Waugh, Huxley and Douglas, as well as such poets as Eliot and Auden, were spearheads of the cultural future, like the society to which they belonged they were also regretting the passing of the past; as Auden says in *Dance of Death*: 'People desiring a new life while secretly longing for the old.'

Those who read their work and identified with them felt the same—hence the cultured traveller's longing for simple fishing villages where one could really get to know the people of the country, and where the people of the country were courteous to the point of servility; for hill towns in which the churches were not listed in the guide book and which could therefore be classed as discoveries; for small inns, as long as they were clean and had reasonable plumbing; and for the picturesque and grateful poor who blessed one for the gift of an old pair of tennis shoes.

The less cultured travellers or tourists of the period between the wars were not readers of Lawrence; indeed, they would have felt extremely shocked by him. And they were less at ease in a foreign environment than their forbears, who had been buoyed up by the knowledge that they belonged to the most powerful nation on earth. Being novices, they did not seek out unusual places but instead stuck to the Cook's Tour where they were safe and knew they would not have any problems with foreign train conductors, customs officers, hoteliers or even the local boatman.

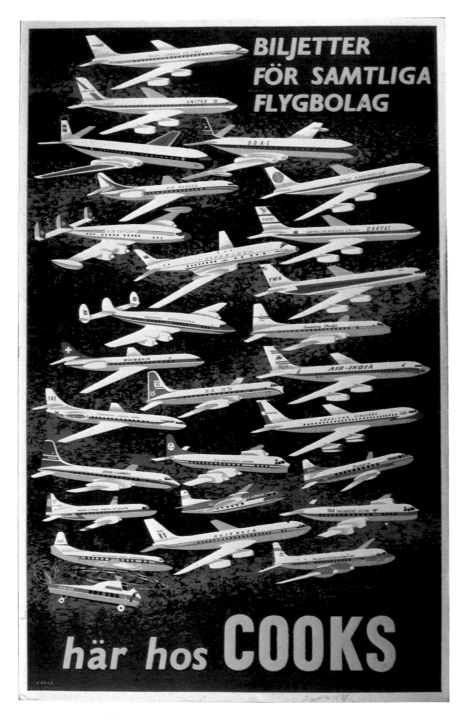

This poster was translated into many different languages
and used in Cook's offices throughout the world to remind
the public of the range of choice available in airlines.

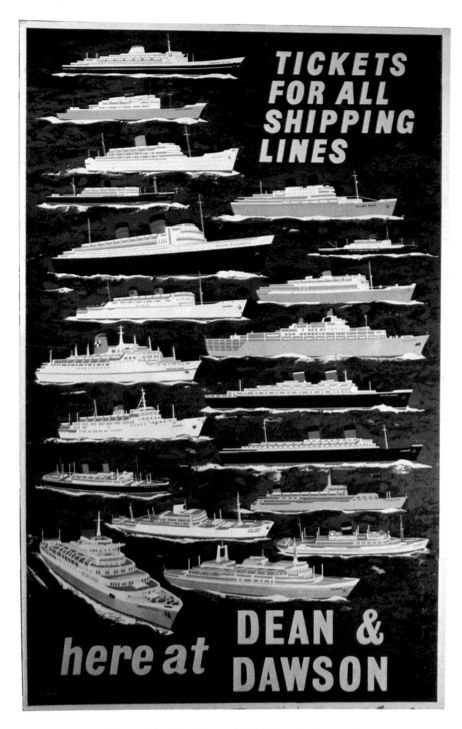

Many of the ships featured in this Dean & Dawson (a
subsidiary of Cook's) poster in the 1950s have disappeared,
but their images are a reminder of the great age of cruising.

A stylish Cook's Tour to St Moritz offered a flight by Imperial Airways and a stay at the Palace Hotel to see the Grand Prix horse race on ice.

These people who represented the growing number of tourists in the period between the wars were the forerunners of the greater invasion of Europe that was to follow after World War II. Most of them travelled to the traditional places—France, Italy, Germany, Switzerland—and by the traditional methods: channel steamer and train. The costs were low, though for people who earned an average salary of £3 per week perhaps not as inexpensive as they seem now. A week in Switzerland cost £8.17s. and an eighteen-day tour of Italy, £25.10s.6d., both fares including travel and hotel.

There were tours farther afield too: Cooks could offer some 2,400 hotels in some 1,200 resorts, all with their special railway ticket and hotel coupon arrangement. Among conducted tours, the 'culture cities' of Europe; the Middle East; and

The German ideals of health and beauty which were much admired throughout Europe gave a new slant to winter sports.

The famous 1936 Olympic Games were designed to show off the supremacy of the master race.

XIth OLYMPIC GAMES AUGUST 1·16th BERLIN GERMANY

● Olympic Year is the World's Festive Year in Germany. The XIth Olympic Games are centered in a grand programme of exciting attractions: The Bayreuth Wagner Festival Plays, the Munich Opera Festivals, International Olympic Art Exhibitions, brilliant theatricals, interesting expositions and conventions. German genius for organization has timed these events so that you can enjoy them during a glorious vacation in Germany. In addition: Scenic grandeur and natural beauty . . . famous health resorts . . . romantic castles . . . picturesque folk festivals . . . medieval towns . . . cosmopolitan cities . . . the Rhine. Modern travel comfort and the traditional hospitality of the land of Wanderlust and Gemütlichkeit. Railroad fares reduced 60% and Registered Travel Marks at low rates. Write for booklet 94.

GERMAN RAILROADS INFORMATION OFFICE
665 Fifth Avenue at 53rd Street, New York

America, ranked high. A favourite tour was to view the battlefields of World War I (cost 20 guineas). A trip to America on the *Mauretania*, *Berengaria* or *Aquitania* cost £30.10s. in cabin class, and the annual round the world tour was available for £1,025.

Since the 1890s, the Cooks had tried to popularize skiing, much to the dismay of Leslie Stephen to whom it seemed that the Swiss valleys were 'bending the knee to Baal' in entertaining tourists. Sir Henry Lunn had managed to get skiing parties going by allying himself with Etonians and Harrovians and thus overcoming the prejudice that potential skiers from the upper levels of the middle classes would have against being part of a tour.

In the 1920s, the prejudice was still there but the number of tourists who wanted to emulate the members of the Alpine Ski Club was increasing and they had no qualms about joining a winter sports tour. Once again, as their grandfather and father had done so often in the past, the Cook grandsons seized the opportunity and began the energetic promotion of ski holidays. Special trains were chartered solely for the use of Cooks tourists, and uniformed representatives accompanied the parties, which as usual consisted of more women than men. The brochure covers of the period have a distinctly feminine appeal and the accent throughout is more on romance than sport.

'Amid much laughter, men, women and kiddies are tumbling and sprawling about in all attitudes on the soft snow,' says a description in the Cooks *Travellers Gazette*, the new name given to *The Excursionist* after the turn of the century. 'For speed and the sheer ecstasy of flight what can be better than the swift rush of a toboggan ... and in the evening "the skaters" lanterns dart hither and thither ... while from the ballroom comes the sound of haunting rhythmic music.'

The message of the winter sports brochures was Romance and Freedom and it accorded with the spirit of the age. In 1928, as already mentioned, the Cook's company passed out of the hands of the Cook family, and Cook's Tours became part of the *Compagnie des Wagons-Lits et des Grands Express Europeens*, to appear in various guises: as motor-coach tours, first introduced as local excursions on solid rubber-tyred buses in Paris in 1903 and in the 1920s extended farther afield—then pneumatic tyres arrives; as chauffeur-driven motor-car tours; and as adventurous tours which followed in the footsteps of nineteenth-century Empire trail-blazers like Burton, Speke, Livingstone and Stanley, as well as those of such popularizers of travel and exploration as Rosita Forbes and Arthur Halliburton.

Among the tours Cooks offered to their adventure-minded clientele were a Cape to Cairo trip (the company refused to make itself responsible for any trophies shot en route); an automobile trip to the desert and the Oasis of Bou-Saada in Algeria, costing 550 French francs; and another more expensive tour through Kabylia to Biskra and the Garden of Allah which for 2,150 French francs took Cooks tourists to Maison Carrée, Alma, Tizi-Ouzou, Bouggie, Cap Carbon, Souk-el-Tenine, the gorges of Chabet, Kerrata, Setif, Constantine, Batna, Timgad, El Kantar, Biskra, Sidi Okba, Bou-Saada, the Gorges of Palestra and Algiers.

The arrangements for motor tours to the Siwa oasis in Libya in 1927 were typical of these African Tours. The contractor was the Libyan Oases Association, and the agreement it came to with the Cooks suggests that the latter were still thinking on the same spacious scale as they had in Egypt in the 1880s.

The Association, apart from supplying motor cars in first-class running order, properly equipped for travelling in the desert, plus back-up cars in case of

Thomas Cook

Far and away ~ the best

in Egypt, Africa, Far East, Indonesia, Australia, Caribbean & the Americas 1975-6

A modern brochure that sells long-distance holidays with comforts undreamt of by Cook's tourists of the nineteenth century.

ABOVE
The cost of flying was high in the 1920s so Cook's tried to persuade the public to take short trips.

ABOVE RIGHT
Apart from the cost, there was also the safety factor to deter tourists from flying.

breakdown, also undertook to provide comfortable and clean sleeping and living accommodation, and four meals a day for the tourists in their care.

Breakfast, even in the middle of the desert, would be properly British: tea or coffee, eggs and bacon or a meat course, toast with butter and marmalade. Lunch would be an hors-d'oeuvre, followed by cold meat with vegetables and salad, plus cheese, fruit and coffee. Dinner would consist of soup, fish, meat, vegetables and salad, plus cheese, fruit and coffee.

Accommodation on the route was also surprisingly lavish. There was a stone-built rest house at Mersa Matrouh, with five bedrooms, dining room and lounge. The bedrooms were properly furnished, and had a zinc dish bath. 'Earth closets will be kept in good order and clean water supplied from a well.'

The same toilet facilities were available in the half-way camp, which had large mess and lounge tents, and double-fly small tents with camp beds and full camp equipment, plus bathroom extensions.

At the Siwa oasis, a proper hotel was built for the tourists. Called the Prince Farouk Hotel, it was built of mud bricks with a palm log roof, 'in proper Siwian style'. This time there were two bathrooms, each with a zinc bath, though the tourists still had to make do with earth closets.

Each party was to have a personal guide and lecturer, at least one of whom would seem to have been a British ex-Army officer, whose job it was to supervise the general arrangements for the comfort of the passengers, and to see that they

To present-day passengers the
interior luxury of Imperial
Airways' aircraft is almost
unbelievable.

ABOVE
The zeppelin presented the
first air challenge to the
transatlantic liners but their
success was short-lived. This
picture shows the SS *New
York* and the *Graf Zeppelin*.

LEFT
Innovations introduced
before World War I came into
popular use after the war.
Charabancs with pneumatic
tyres were used for the first
coach tours.

Imperial Airways began flights to Australia using three or four types of aircraft for different stages of the journey. The Scylla type took passengers on the first stage.

extracted from the tour 'the utmost enjoyment and profit'.

The garages approached for these and Cooks many other motoring tours were scattered far and wide around the world, from the Eastern Garage in Shanghai to Monsieur Emile's in Nice. In the latter's contract, it was clearly stated that he was responsible for providing care with up-to-date, comfortable seating accommodation which 'shall have a hood and waterproof side covers to protect passengers against bad weather and the driver should wear suitable uniform'.

The greatest adventure of all was, of course, flight. During their last decade with the company, the Cook family introduced this latest innovation in transport with the same enthusiasm and confidence with which Thomas Cook had introduced his first train excursion eighty years earlier.

This was not the company's first venture into tourism in the air. In 1911, for instance, they had made an agreement with the *Compagnie Générale Transarienne à Lucerne*, to sell tickets for excursions in the airship *Ville de Lucerne* round Lucerne and round Burgenstock and the Righi. Cooks were to receive six per cent commission on every passenger who booked through the company.

The first Cooks' advertisement offering aeroplane flights appeared in *The Times* in 1919. It offered just a joy ride, but within a year the company published a brochure, *Aerial Travel for Business or Pleasure*, which offered flights in converted war-time Handley Page bombers.

Aware that the public were frightened of this new means of transport, the Cooks did their best to persuade them that there was nothing to fear.

'The Handley Page is the largest aeroplane in existence,' they wrote, 'and probably the most widely known of machines. Built as a night bomber to fly long distance it was designed mainly with a view to safety and reliability ...' The brochure continues in the same soothing way throughout, pointing out that it is not designed for trick flying: 'the pilot will not loop the loop or perform any other spectacular but useless and dangerous stunts.'

The journey to Paris took two hours and fifty minutes and cost £10, with Cooks

ROUND THE WORLD TOURS

THOS COOK & SON.

Round the World tours were a regular part of the Cook's programme though the numbers involved were small.

ABOVE
India—the jewel in the Crown of Empire—was also an important part of the Cook's Empire.

THE AMERICAN TRAVELER'S GAZETTE

20

"A great trip, Bill, something that still ranks as adventure . . ."

Bringing AFRICA Home

The first Cook's tourists to Africa felt that they too were like the explorers who had preceded them by only a decade or two.

Wherever railways were established the Cook's Tour followed. The Victorian Railways air-conditioned, all-steel, streamlined train, made travel in Australia as comfortable as anywhere in the world.

offering a number of alternative companies, among which were Imperial Airways (formed in 1924), Air Union, Messageries Aeriennes and KLM.

There were few passengers and competition was fierce, so the air companies began to offer incentives in the same way that hotels and resorts engaged in the tourist trade did. Passengers were taken to the airport by limousine, and escorted to the aircraft, where they were provided with a comfortable wicker chair. There were no lavatory facilities to start with nor cabin service, but food began to appear and by 1927 a full menu was served.

The Cooks' quick reaction to the possibility of using air transport to carry their passengers was not confined to Britain, and the brothers now set out all over the world to make contracts with everyone operating an airline.

In the United States commercial flying had begun with the mails and the pilots were often involved in hair-raising incidents as they crossed the Rocky Mountains and other wild terrain. Passenger flying began in America in 1926 and developed fast as it was the most convenient way to traverse the huge continent. Among the companies the Cooks approached in the United States were the Mercury Aviation Company of California, the Curtiss Flying Station at Atlantic City, and the Aeromarine Sightseeing and Navigation Company of Delaware. Contractual conditions were similar with all three, the Cooks offering to canvass for passengers and sell tickets, and leaving the airlines to be responsible for running the aircraft.

'The contractor agrees,' ran the Cooks' contract, 'that all aircraft and other vehicles used by it should be in every way suitable for the service required, well appointed, well engined, in sound condition throughout and operated and manned and controlled by duly qualified men and that the aircraft and all persons employed in connection therewith shall be provided with a proper licence.'

In 1929, the year after the last two members of the Cook family, Frank and Ernest, retired from the business, Cooks arranged the first tour by charter aircraft. This was a special party from New York to Chicago to attend the Dempsey-Tunney heavyweight boxing championship. Sherry's Restaurant in New York provided the lunch boxes, and the trip was completely successful.

COMPAGNIE GÉNÉRALE
TRANSSAHARIENNE

48, Boulevard Gallieni
ISSY-LES-MOULINEAUX (Seine)

Adresse Télégraphique
TRANSSAHARIENNE-ISSY-LES-MOULINEAUX

ARRIVÉE D'UNE VOITURE COUCHETTE
AU BORDJ DE REGGAN

Service Automobile
COLOMB-BÉCHAR-
─── GAO ───

Travel in hitherto inaccessible parts of the world became possible for anyone with money in the 1920s. The Cooks made contracts with adventurous contractors such as the Compagnie General Transsaharienne and took passengers across the Sahara on cars fitted with metal tracks.

The greatest benefit to be derived from flying was the saving of time, and the airlines never ceased to point out how much faster it was to travel by air than by other means. The early aircraft could not compete with ocean liners on the Atlantic crossing, one of the most lucrative routes on earth. Zeppelins could, however, and did.

For seven glorious years German zeppelins were masters of the Atlantic, running regular services at first to Rio de Janeiro and then to North America.

The *Graf Zeppelin*, which was advertised in Cooks' brochures, made its first flight in 1928. After cruising to America and the Middle East, it made a round-the-world flight in 1929 before settling down to a regular run to South America. It was a huge airship and an unforgettable sight to those who saw it, comparable to a clipper in full sail. The similarity with a ship was accentuated by its promenade deck and its twenty-five two-berth cabins on the upper deck. In addition, there were richly decorated public rooms and a smoking room where surveillance was intense, for any kind of open flame was a danger to the airship.

The concept of the airships was magnificent but, as the explosion of the *Graf Zeppelin*'s sister ship *Hindenburg* at Lakehurst, New Jersey, and the accident to the British R101 at Beauvais showed, they could be dangerous. The problem of commercial flights across oceans remained temporarily unsolved.

Long-distance flying to and from the East did not present a problem, for the trip could be undertaken in easy stages with overnight stops at Athens, Gaza, Basra and Sharjah, as Imperial Airways did in 1927, later extending the run to Australia in 1934. Nor was it difficult to run a flight to South Africa because there were plenty of stops en route, but how to get across the Atlantic?

The mountains of Austria and Switzerland were seen in a rosy, romantic glow by the tourists of the 1930s. Being close to nature meant walking, canoeing and cycling through Alpine valleys.

Imperial Airways and Pan American had decided to experiment with flying boats early in the 1930s. Like the airships, the flying boats were a superb concept. They were giants of the air, with a spaciousness that is difficult to imagine today. The interior was divided into compartments in each of which there were four armchairs with plenty of leg room and in which a table was set up at meal times. There was a small promenade deck, and on the Pan American clippers it was possible to retire to a berth during the long night flights across the Pacific.

The only snags were that they were not able to fly long distances without landing for refuelling and they were vulnerable to the state of the sea that was their landing strip. They were used considerably for air holidays, however, and there are advertisements showing their service to Madeira, the Mediterranean and other destinations. In 1939, the Cooks took the plunge and advertised a tour round the world by flying boat. The *Yankee Clipper* would take off from Southampton and cross the Atlantic to New York. Passengers would then fly across the United States via Salt Lake City and cross the Pacific by another Pan Am flying boat to Hong Kong where they would fly back to Britain by Imperial Airways. Price, £475 for thirty days. But it was only the rich Cooks tourists who could afford air holidays.

Then came a breakthrough: the Holidays with Pay Act in 1938 enabled the Ministry of Labour to bring about paid holidays by agreement with employers. The following year Cooks made arrangements with BEA to charter an aircraft and to quote an inclusive price for a holiday to the South of France.

The air package holiday had been born; but the war brought it quickly to an end, and it was not until 1955 that it was revived again.

CHAPTER ELEVEN

Cheaper
by the Million

The Holidays with Pay Act of 1938 meant that by the end of the war some 14 million people in Britain were entitled to paid holidays.

A great new market for holidays had been born, and all those people who had been deprived of holiday enjoyment—and plentiful food—for the five war years were eager to experience it. Holidays at home prospered immediately: all the seashores that were available to the public, and which were not out of bounds because of mines and barbed wire entanglements, became packed with tourists and day trippers. Bicycling, a tourist craze that had taken off in the 1890s when Cooks encouraged ladies to cycle in Normandy and arranged for their clothes to be sent on ahead so that they could change into their long skirts on arrival at their hotel, became a popular activity again. Cheap accommodation was provided in holiday camps like Filey and Prestatyn (built by the London North Eastern Railway immediately before the war), and came under Cooks ownership when the company was bought by the railways.

Foreign travel could not begin immediately, for the damage to communications with hotels and resorts had to be repaired, and arrangements had to be made regarding rates of exchange between countries. In October 1945 a basic foreign allowance was announced in Britain; every adult could spend £100 abroad and every child £50. This was for expenditure overseas and did not include transport on British trains, aircraft or ships.

In November of the same year a headline in the *Evening Standard* cried out 'Plenty of Swiss food awaits the British Tourist. We are anxious to share it'. Here was temptation indeed for a population that had put up for years with food rationing and shortages. After the ban on private visits was lifted in April 1946, 200,000 tourists crossed the Channel during the summer. Within months, there were the usual carping complaints about the behaviour of British tourists abroad, including one from Collie Knox the *Daily Mail* columnist.

From what little I have seen of my fellow countrymen and women in Switzerland—though that little is more than enough—I cannot hail most of them as type-cast ambassadors of Empire . . . The best 'goods' are obviously not getting through. Most of the 'goods' here talk too loudly, eat too much and make any self-respecting Englishman writhe with embarrassment.

Cooks were not slow off the mark in this rush to the country whose tourist trade they had fostered. Soon there were tours by train for a mere £12.4s.6d., and, in the tradition of the post-World War I tours, there were tours to the battlefields.

During the war the company had been reduced in size, though brochures offering holidays to regions outside the war zones continued to appear, without, strangely enough, any reference to the conflict at all. Those of the staff who

The tourist map as it looked in 1950. The Costa del Sol and Costa Blanca in Spain had not yet been developed, nor the Algarve in Portugal, and many of the resorts named were still small villages.

remained at work were by no means idle, for besides arranging for the evacuation of children during the 'phoney' war and after the air raids started, Cooks operated a letter service through Portugal for people left behind the enemy lines, and lent its extensive Egyptian shipyards for the servicing and repairs of boats of all kinds, and its mechanical workshops for the repair and maintenance of vehicles engaged in the East Africa operations. The company also despatched to Britons behind the lines some 700,000 food parcels subscribed for by its customers.

In 1946, it was back to the business of tourism again and the Cook's Tours were recreated to serve the 750,000 people who wanted to go abroad in 1947. The tone of the brochures was now frankly romantic and hedonistic.

'Dreams of Delight' one was headed. 'Just for a few idle moments give yourself over to day dreaming. Imagine yourself holiday making in Switzerland. You see yourself basking in the sunshine besides some shimmering lake that reflects the beauty of the surrounding snow capped mountains . . .'

This hypnotic approach was designed, as ever, for women and it was an instant success. Ten days in Lucerne cost £18.15s.6d., with accommodation in splendid rococo hotels straight out of Ruritania. The formula was irresistible.

The following year Cooks were offering air tours to the French Riviera by Air France and Sabena, at a cost of £48.14s.6d. for ten days at Menton; and for only £25.14s.6d. one could fly to Trouville. In 1948 the night sleeper to Paris was

reinstated and travel to Paris in this luxurious pre-war manner, staying at a hotel for nine days, cost £27. 17s.

To deal with the fast-growing new traffic the tour companies revived the charter train principle established by Thomas Cook on his first tour. A group of leading agents including Cooks who banded together to buy transport in bulk under the name of Creative Tour Agents Conference, chartered trains to Switzerland, Italy, Southern France and Catalan Spain. These were the farthest limits accessible within twenty-four hours by rail; further would have meant two nights in a train and it was thought that this would be unacceptable to the public.

This was the high point of the Cook's Tour: never had so many people travelled by train on their holidays overseas. Every day of the week, but especially at weekends, Victoria and Waterloo stations in London were crowded with tourists waiting for their leaders to appear. In the case of Cooks, these were tall men in dark blue uniforms with as much gold braid as naval officers, while other travel agents — and with the growth of the business they were sprouting like dragons' teeth — put into the field a variety of guides and mentors from students on holiday to wizened middle-aged men of uncertain identity. Lists of names fluttered in their hands as they called out for their charges, many of whom preferred not to identify themselves as members of a group.

Finally the trains slid out of the stations towards the Channel port where another

The Promenade des Anglais, Nice, once the place where the English leisured class strolled, became indistinguishable from Brighton or Eastbourne as the post-war travel boom took off.

breathless half hour was spent in moving from the train to the ship. It was only a Channel crossing but for most people it was a journey full of excitement, with the seagulls wheeling overhead, the smell of sea, tar and oil heavy in the air, and the blue sweatered sailors offering to carry luggage and guaranteeing to get one off the ship first on the French side.

There was still much of the communal spirit of wartime in these tourist crowds, and unlike the taciturn air passengers of today, everyone talked to everyone else, sharing the pleasures of a good crossing or the horrors of a bad one.

On the French side, there was a rush down the gangway, with those who had tipped their sailor profiting from his knowledge of which side the ship would berth, to the grey-green trains that stood like motionless elephants on every available siding. Customs and passports formalities took place on the train which then headed for Paris, where those going south changed trains for the long ride through the night. There was a magic in leaving the suburbs of Paris at dusk and finding oneself in the olive vineyards and dry earth of the south in the morning. It was an enchantment accentuated by the smell of hot coffee and croissants for which everyone queued as they had queued the night before for their supper, unless they had a good courier with influence.

Then came that first glimpse of the Mediterranean, blue, breath-catching as an approaching love affair (which it was).

A big problem for those who were in the business of satisfying the demand for foreign holidays was that there were few suitable hotels. There were *pensions*, and

Those who did not travel by
train went by coach and
enjoyed the gregariousness of
a coach tour party.

there were those vast rococo palaces built for the *Belle Epoque*, and nothing much else between. The *pensions*, run by hospitable, helpful families who had little idea about making a pot of tea and even less about plain boiled vegetables, were a source of anxiety to the representatives of the tour companies. The grand hotels that thought the new guests were like the ones they had been built for were a source of concern for the tourists.

These great buildings, designed on a lavish scale with family suites, could, when the suites were broken down into rooms, accommodate several hundred guests. There were no longer hundreds of guests of the type they sought, however, so the populations of the grand hotels became more and more mixed. There were the older clients, rich ladies from Milan, or Madrid, or Lyons who would install themselves for a month or two and receive a steady stream of relatives who gathered themselves around them as if they were sitting for a picture by Winterhalter. There were the distinguished foreign visitors who seemed unaware that times were changing, the new industrialists with their courtesans, the English bourgeoisie, and there were the workers from Ford, the crane drivers, the oil mechanics and other representatives of the new society who were amazed or pugnacious, according to their temperament, at

Many of the coach tour passengers were from overseas. The coach tour
provided them with an opportunity to see a great deal of Europe on what
for many of them was really the journey of a lifetime.

The Swiss Alps had lost none of their attraction after over one hundred
years as a tourist destination, only now distant views could be brought
closer by the slot telescope.

The British began the fashion for bathing and relaxation and they were followed by Germans, French, Scandinavians and many others. Even Eastern European countries let their hair down occasionally as can be seen here, in the wave bath at the St Gellew Hotel, Budapest.

finding themselves on a holiday in a place that resembled the Albert Hall.

The new classless society managed surprisingly well in these relics of Edwardian grandeur, and apart from such obvious examples of culture clash as women in curlers and men in sandals and sock suspenders next to couples groomed for a club dinner, the new society showed signs of succeeding.

As the years wore on, however, it was noticeable that the young drifted away to a new, custom-built type of resort and the curlers disappeared to be replaced by bouffant hairstyles coiffeured by a village lass who had studied in London.

Despite the obvious signs of a burgeoning new business, there was at first little investment capital available to those in the tour business. This soon changed, and in the empty ground in and around the seashore villages, grey reinforced-concrete pillars began to sprout like space-age plants. Breeze blocks and bricks were soon hidden under a smooth layer of plaster from which the sun ricocheted in blinding whiteness.

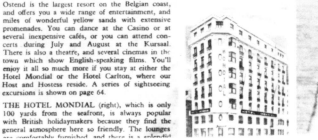

From £13. 18s.

Gay Colourful
OSTEND

WESTENDE

Not far from the gaiety and bright lights of Ostend is Westende, a delightful little resort which is another good choice for the family holiday. You can bathe in safety from its wonderful sandy beach. Our offers range from £19 3s. for an 8-day holiday, and £32 1s. for a 15-day holiday.

Ostend is the largest resort on the Belgian coast, and offers you a wide range of entertainment, and miles of wonderful yellow sands with extensive promenades. You can dance at the Casino or at several inexpensive cafés, or you can attend concerts during July and August at the Kursaal. There is also a theatre, and several cinemas in the town which show English-speaking films. You'll enjoy it all so much more if you stay at either the Hotel Mondial or the Hotel Carlton, where our Host and Hostess reside. A series of sightseeing excursions is shown on page 64.

THE HOTEL MONDIAL (right), which is only 100 yards from the seafront, is always popular with British holidaymakers because they find the general atmosphere here so friendly. The lounges are comfortably furnished, and there is a splendid

---

'Gay colourful Ostend' was all right as long as tourists could not afford to go further south, but with the advent of cheap Mediterranean holidays, many people deserted the resorts nearest home.

The new buildings had few reminders of the past which was anathema to the iconoclastic fifties: here and there, perhaps, a gilded mirror, a painted chest, a carved table, like a museum piece, reassuringly dead. The rest had featureless spaciousness in which a new society could evolve in guiltless comfort. The new hotels were like television and film sets, a bit tawdry and insubstantial in the broad light of day but totally persuasive in the illumination contrived to show them off.

The new tourist cut himself off more and more from the past, and excursions to historic places were reserved for a dull day or when the extent of the sunburn counselled a day in the shade. Baedeker and Cooks' *Guides* were replaced by handy digests in which information was dispensed briefly between the photographs.

The natives of the tourist regions, accustomed to modest numbers of earnest middle-class travellers, were stunned by the abundance of British visitors, who still outnumbered all other nationalities. The older people had been servants to the pre-war long-term visitors and they treated the new tourists with the same respect as they had their old masters. But the younger ones, particularly the men, quickly picked up the attitudes of their guests. The ideas of liberal Britain spread like wildfire, and as it entered the jet age, the tourist scene that had remained relatively unchanged since the beginning of the Cook's Tour became unrecognizable.

174

CHAPTER TWELVE

The Jet Age

In ancient times the journey of a comet across the heavens was an event full of omens and portents and when the Comet jet aircraft made the first commercial flight from London to Johannesburg in 1952 it was regarded similarly as a fateful event.

Most of the airlines of the world had until this moment been building up their fleets with piston-engined or turbo-prop aircraft to deal with the increasing air traffic, which had grown from about twenty million (eighty per cent of it in Europe and America) to over sixty million in seven years. The Comet was the first British jet (operated only over land routes), closely followed by the Boeing 707, first across the Atlantic in 1958; and the airlines were faced with the need to buy jets, which though faster and cheaper to operate, were more expensive to buy, at a time when they had invested heavily in turbo-props.

By the 1950s, the holiday tours market in Britain had grown considerably with some three million people travelling out of the country every year, as well as an annual Transatlantic traffic of about one million. Most of these people still travelled by train and steamship, for the cost of air travel was still prohibitive for the average traveller. An uncertain start had been made in providing cheap air holidays by combining flights in old aircraft with economical accommodation in tents, notably by Vladimir Raitz, who later created the Horizon company, the success and failure of which were notable events in the development of the package tour. The public as a whole lacked confidence in flying under these conditions. The availability of reliable, brand-new aircraft turned the tide.

Cooks, who had already pioneered air package holidays to the South of France in 1939, only to be stopped by the outbreak of war, now revived the idea of Cook's Tours by air, offering 14 days on the Riviera for £59.12s.6d.

Changes in transport and competition from rivals had always been successfully surmounted by the company, ever since Thomas Cook had been faced by the undercutting activities of rival railway companies, and Cooks were confident that they could ride the new wave to success. This time, however, the circumstances were different.

Over the years, Thomas Cook had become an institution associated in the public mind with Empire and the Establishment, but in the fifties this was more of a handicap than an asset with the consumer society, especially its younger members, who formed the basis of a new consumer market rapidly exploited by the fashion, catering and cosmetic trades.

Cooks, trapped by their traditional image and the tastes of their conventional middle-class clientele, had little room to manoeuvre against the new companies that jetted into the travel scene, free of traditional encumbrances and able to project an image that seemed to define the new start that the public sought. In addition, Cooks had been nationalized in 1948 and risk money for a state-owned organization became

The flying boat seemed the answer to long-distance flying between 1928 and 1950, but it was soon displaced by the increased range of land-based aircraft.

impossible to obtain. They therefore did not take part in the movement towards vertical integration, that is buying their own airline with which to run their holidays cheaply as did Thomson Holidays, who own Britannia Airways, or Cosmos who own Monarch.

The new spirit of the decade was reflected in books like *Room at the Top*, films like *I'm All Right Jack* and slogans like 'You've never had it so good'. The new society did not want to know about the past; it threw all the old middle-class, emotive words like duty, patriotism, honour and responsibility out of the window, believing they were the fraudulent coinage of an unacceptable society. In these circumstances, Cooks and all the well-known names of the travel industry who had pioneered popular travel in the late nineteenth century, struggled, merged with other companies, or disappeared entirely. Sir Henry Lunn popularized Lunns to compromise with the new ethos; Polytechnic, Frames and Workers Travel became shadows of their former selves and in their place arose the new names, Clarksons, Cosmos, Horizon and many others.

In the free market, the entrepreneurs multiplied like flies on sugar. The more they multiplied, the less sugar there was for everyone. Moreover, other factors were changing the face of the holiday tour business.

In the early days of the post-war travel explosion, continental hoteliers, whose major clients were British, were accustomed to providing rooms without thought of payment until the room had been occupied. Life was not too difficult for them; many of them ran the hotels with their families, labour was cheap and food was plentiful, and twenty per cent occupancy kept the hotels out of insolvency. As the post-war period developed, however, they came under the pressure of the changing times; staff became more difficult to find as the young took up more lucrative and less exacting work in industry, and those who did remain in catering demanded shorter

BOAC luggage label showing the extent of the air routes in 1950. The war brought about great technological advances in flying and the development of aircraft like the Boeing Stratocruiser and the Douglas DC 6B.

hours, thus creating a need for more staff. Food prices went up and foreign tour operators demanded that prices should go down—in return for which they promised more customers.

Thus, hoteliers were caught in the ever-quickening spiral of rising costs. The answer was more rooms, often impossible to add to existing structures. This led to new building, for which loans were necessary, and a new burden of loan interest was added to already increasing costs. Fighting back, the hotelier began to look around for other markets and found them in the growth of holiday tourism from Germany and Scandinavia and later from other countries as international tourism grew. Now, the hotelier began to demand payment in advance from his customers for the rooms set aside for prospective guests and, since many of these often did not show up, he began to overbook as well, as a matter of course.

More and more individual hoteliers could not stand the pace and merged with others or were swallowed up by large conglomerates who appointed executives to look after the vast establishments, which were now increasing their rooms, often to over one thousand bedrooms. The hotel business had become big industry: a vast series of factories catering for the ever-increasing public demand.

The power house of the world's greatest post-war industry was, of course, the means of transport, just as it had been in the nineteenth century when the establishment of the railways led to the development of resorts in Britain and then in the rest of the world.

At first, spheres of operation were clearly defined. The airlines ran their services and the tour operators ran the tours, using the air services for transport. When aircraft were available they were chartered for flights to particular destinations; as the traffic increased they were chartered for a whole series of holidays, with the price reduced accordingly. To enjoy the privileges of a charter it was, under British law,

Old style hotels also profited
from the jet age holiday rush
and some managed to
maintain their traditional
cachet while modernising
their interiors to keep up with
the new standards expected.

obligatory to be a member of a bona fide group or society travelling together for a particular purpose. This led to the growth of a strange assortment of societies whose only *raison d'etre* was that they offered cheap flights.

The main development of the holiday charter system was through the regular tour company channels. The charter, which guaranteed a certain price to the airline, was a profitable business for the holiday company only as long as it could operate with aircraft as full as possible. This was not always feasible, for an aircraft transporting a group of people to a certain destination might be obliged to return empty. Thus, the time charter idea was born. By this system, the tour company had use of an aircraft for a period of time it chose, so long as this accorded with the overall scheduling of flights along international corridors. This meant that once a group of passengers had been deposited at one point, the aircraft could then undertake another commitment or extend its flight to a second destination.

The success of the charters created a problem for the scheduled airlines, as soon there were air companies in formation which had none of the onerous obligations of running regular services, so the scheduled airlines went into the charter business in a bigger way than before. British Airways created its Silver Wing Services solely to provide for the growing holiday tour market. Freddie Laker, who had been managing director of the failed British United Airways, set up on his own as a charter operator. In Europe, Air France, Lufthansa, Alitalia and Iberia set up their own charter hire companies and a new air travel stratum of operations grew.

During the sixties and seventies the battle between scheduled airlines and tour charter companies continued. Advanced Booking Charters (ABCs), which provide cheap fares but are limited to those who book in advance, were answered by the regular airlines' Advanced Booking Excursion fare which offers a similar arrangement but on regular flights instead of the more limited dates of the ABCs. A challenge to both systems was set up by Laker with his standby flights and this, in turn, was immediately answered by the regular airlines with standby flights of their own. However, mounting competitive pressure, aggravated by the current economic recession, finally obliged Laker to put his airline into the hands of the Receiver in February 1982.

In the ding-dong battle to keep hold of their precious markets, the airlines have run into deep financial problems, which have lead them into the exploration of other

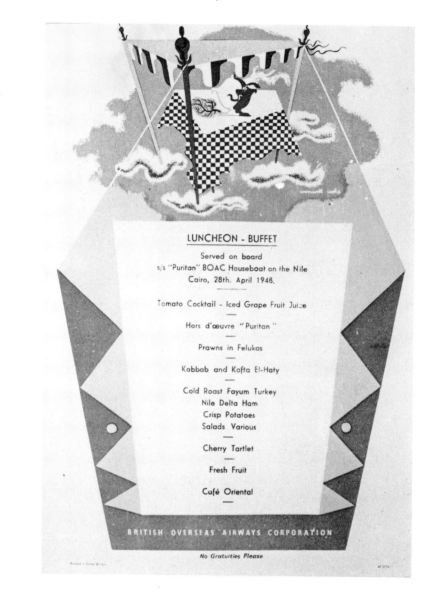

LUNCHEON - BUFFET

Served on board
s/s "Puritan" BOAC Houseboat on the Nile
Cairo, 28th. April 1948.

Tomato Cocktail - Iced Grape Fruit Juice

Hors d'œuvre "Puritan"

Prawns in Felukas

Kabbab and Kofta El-Haty

Cold Roast Fayum Turkey
Nile Delta Ham
Crisp Potatoes
Salads Various

Cherry Tartlet

Fresh Fruit

Café Oriental

BRITISH OVERSEAS AIRWAYS CORPORATION

No Gratuities Please

Meals in flight became the rule in the 1950s but before this hot food was served on flying boats. On the first flight to South Africa the BOAC inaugural passengers were treated to meals on land, or, as in the case of this period design menu, on the BOAC houseboat during a Cairo stopover.

revenue-earning activities. Many of these have meant that they are challenging their own clients, the tour operator and travel agent. Many airlines run their own tour-operating programmes, offering holidays under their own brand names such as Sovereign, Enterprise, etc.

The problems of the hotel and airline business are universal and though price-cutting wars and discounting have benefited the consumer, the existing situation may not be to their advantage in the long run. It is plain to see that the business of travel has become a volume business, but it is still handled in a fragmented manner.

Because of free-enterprise ideology, too many competitive units are permitted to enter the market to prove their right to survival. Once in, however, there is a reluctance to let natural forces take their course, for this would strike a blow at the

With the jet age there came to an end the cultural motivation for travel and the message changed to sun, sand and sex.

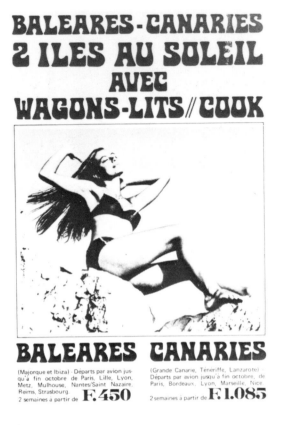

BALEARES-CANARIES 2 ILES AU SOLEIL AVEC WAGONS-LITS//COOK

BALEARES CANARIES

(Majorque et Ibiza) · Départs par avion jus-qu'à fin octobre de Paris, Lille, Lyon, Metz, Mulhouse, Nantes/Saint Nazaire, Reims, Strasbourg. 2 semaines à partir de **F.450**

(Grande Canarie, Ténériffe, Lanzarote) · Départs par avion jusqu'à fin octobre, de Paris, Bordeaux, Lyon, Marseille, Nice. 2 semaines à partir de **F.1.085**

industry, causing unemployment and jeopardizing the investment capital borrowed from banks and finance houses. Moreover, many of the world's travel and tourist facilities are heavily subsidized by individual governments, thus distorting the workings of a free world market.

Despite the apparent confusion in the world of leisure travel, there is an irresistible tide moving the industry towards larger units, with greater pooling of information and resources. For years now there has been an increasing tendency to develop large-scale resorts such as Torremolinos, Palma Majorca, Rimini and La Grande Motte, and to create purpose-built complexes such as Vilamoura in the Algarve which is being built from scratch to include a yacht harbour, casino and shopping centre as well as large-scale hotels and individual residential blocks with their own private recreation centres.

This rational development of a growing industry is not without its enemies. They of course would prefer to retain some of the old, individualistic character of the leisure business. For such people there are still villages to be found by the sea where the lobster pots and fishing nets decorate the quays, but in these the price of a holiday is higher than in the big resorts and the amenities fewer. Perhaps this will lead back to the old class division which existed in holidays in Victorian times, with the new meritocracy staying at the small traditional resorts where the expensive hotels have individual characters.

As far as the mass of holiday tourists is concerned, it is predictable that economy of size will be more attractive than picturesqueness.

"Why can't Charles and Lady Di board the Britannia from Spain—Spain really IS a British colony!"

This recent cartoon by Cummings is a reminder that Cook's opened up the Spanish coastal resorts in the immediate post-war period, and in fact introduced holidays to Spain in the 1880s.

Economy of size is a concept about which travel agents are becoming more and more aware. Until recently, the retail travel business (except for Thomas Cook), has been operated by individual shopkeepers who, by keeping their overheads down, managed to make a reasonable living from the commissions paid by principals to agents. The increase in the development of large retail chains selling other goods and services as well as travel in their range, has caused a flurry of concern in the industry. When Thomas Cook was acquired by the Midland Bank in 1974 it was thought that this would immediately enlarge the travel company's network by the number of the bank's branches. This has not happened yet, but it could, if competitive pressures were strong enough.

Economy of size is a concept of vital significance in the information, communication and marketing aspects of the travel industry. New technology including the microchip have made it possible to store and make instantly available all the information necessary in the operation of a business. For a service industry such as travel the new systems are essential; they are also expensive to install and therefore only large, well-capitalized organizations can afford to commit themselves to such investments for only long-term benefits. This poses a serious problem for the thousands of small retail travel shops who cannot afford to install instant booking and information systems, and who will, therefore, have to pay rental charges for the use of systems set up by principals or the larger travel agents. It could be, of course, that principals may find it worthwhile to provide these services at a nominal cost in return for an exclusivity; thus, one might find the retail industry set up like the

Millions of tourists converted hitherto poverty-stricken, uncivilised stretches of low-lying coast into clean, well-maintained pleasuredromes.

motor industry with special dealers for each airline, hotel group and other ancillary services.

Time will tell. At the moment the industry created by Thomas Cook, like the transport and catering industries that it serves, is in a turmoil. The Association of British Travel Agents which began its life at the Thomas Cook company headquarters, is at odds with itself, and the control which it once exercised over the conduct of the trade is fast slipping through its fingers, just as the International Air Transport Association's power to protect and regulate the operations of its member airlines is also collapsing under the struggles for survival of individual airlines.

Travel, whether in the shape of the Cook's Tour concept, or in other guises, goes on and the desire to be involved in the world's most dynamic industry is spreading through the western, communist and third worlds like a tidal wave.

CHAPTER THIRTEEN

Paradise Lost

The idea of making travel easily and cheaply available to everyone has always carried with it ethical undertones. Possibly this is because the pioneers of travel for the millions were nearly all motivated by religious and social ideals, and also because the early tourists of whom there were few in relation to the whole working population felt that the enjoyment of leisure required some justification.

During the period of the popularity of holidays at mineral spas, visitors to these watering places disguised their true motives for being there by a pretended concern for their health. This same justification was used when sea bathing became popular. Visits to the continent were excused on similar grounds when the journey included a stay at a spa, but holidays in foreign cities were justified on cultural grounds.

This particular excuse gained ground until World War II, except among the sophisticates who spent holidays at Monte Carlo or bathed on the Côte d'Azur in summer. Thus, in brochures of the between-the-wars period one is offered every conceivable kind of cultural excursion from the ruins of ancient Rome to the caves of Altamira. There were even more exotic and farther afield cultural journeys to enjoy, of course, but not many could afford them.

The idea grew, therefore, that people who travelled in the early years of tourism were all somehow motivated by a thirst for culture and as mentioned previously, this seemed to be born out by the success of such voluminous guide books as those produced by Messrs Baedeker, Murray and by Thomas Cook himself. By contrast, the post-war tourist has appeared a barbaric creature hardly knowing the difference between Venice and Vienna.

Inevitably, this has produced in certain people a nostalgia for a halcyon age when tourists were well-read, well-behaved and culturally improved as a result of their foreign travels.

But did this age really exist? Certainly, more people read detailed guidebooks than they do today; even the smallest pocket book had a limited readership, and certainly a large number of journals were kept throughout holidays and some of them were even published. But would those who kept up these activities have done so had they had the temptations of the various entertainments offered tourists today?

The evidence suggests that beneath the formal demands of the society they lived in tourists then were very much like tourists now. They enjoyed the freedom which they could allow themselves away from the domestic environment, they revelled in the attentions of foreign Romeos, they swooned romantically at scenery, they complained about the food, they distrusted foreigners and when it was over they were glad to get back.

The main difference between tourists in the days of the Cook's Tour and today lies in their numbers. A few tourists acting with abandon one hundred years ago would hardly have been noticed except by the eagle eyes of British residents like

A man-made resort at La Grande Motte in southern France. This was developed in a formerly flat, unattractive coast plagued by mosquitoes and is now a successful holiday region.

O'Dowd or Leslie Stephen who felt affronted at the arrival of ordinary people in lands over which they had a proprietorial interest. But thousands carrying on in the same way today make their mark: the fact that they act and dress in much the same way as they would at home looks incongruous to the more sophisticated traveller abroad and their insistence on a menu suited to their tastes has created the so-called 'international' menu which is anathema to all those who enjoy genuine local cooking.

It is not only in the catering field that the modern tourist's influence is felt. The design of resorts and hotels, the entertainments, the souvenir shops, all reveal the influence of market tastes. The travel agent, formerly a leader of public taste, has become the provider for its satisfaction.

'Sun, Sand, Sea and Sex' the brochures announce in all their more-colourful-than-life photographs, and those who think nostalgically of the Mediterranean of Durrell, Douglas, and Lawrence, sigh with despair. But in one sense the cultural interchange of visitor and host has intensified, though it may not be for the best.

In the pre-World War II Cook's Tour the tourist was insulated from the foreign environment in three ways: first, by his social superiority which established a master-servant relationship between himself and those who served him; secondly, by the vast number of protective servants who surrounded him; and thirdly by the hotels, steamers or other places in which he was accommodated and which bore little relationship to the places in which the natives of the country lived.

Today, though the tourist may live in an artificial village created for his enjoyment, he is no longer a *milord*, and those who serve him, by the process of democratization which the tourists of several generations have helped to introduce, no longer display that servility which flattered the Victorian and Edwardian tourist. What contact exists is therefore more real. It is between ordinary people at an ordinary level and about the common problems of life shared by all mankind. The effect of the grass roots contact of the visiting tourist and the host servant should, therefore, not be underestimated, nor do those countries which try to maintain a strict control of the thoughts and attitudes of their population do so. Franco was not keen to allow tourism into Spain, but when the first British tourists began to arrive in the 1950s the effect on the thoughts and attitudes of young Spaniards was dramatic. In Italy, Greece, Portugal and other Mediterranean countries the waves of young British tourists coming from a society that was itself undergoing a social revolution altered ways of life which had been set in a formal pattern for generations.

There is an effect in the opposite direction too. As a result of the exposure to foreign ways for millions of British people, foreign foods became acceptable in the 'land of beef and two veg', fashion reflected the styles of Continental countries, films from Italy and France found a wider audience and the media devoted more and more attention to what had become a subject of widespread interest.

But to those people who believe that interest in foreign travel should lie in the arts, history and sociology of the countries visited, the tourist Utopia, in which time would be spent usefully and everyone would become more knowledgeable about the world, has not come to pass. It may seem to them that in this respect paradise has been lost.

The other hope of the pioneers of tourism was that it would bring wealth and happiness to countries whose standards of living were inferior to those of the visitors. In modern times this concept has come to include the touring countries

These apartments at La Grande Motte provide for the increasing number of self-catering holidaymakers. They provide highly efficient units for the weekly or fortnightly turnover of mass market traffic.

BELOW
Winter sports look to the future at Flaine. No picturesque chalets here but city-style units built above the summer snowline to provide almost all-the-year-round winter sports holidays.

Processing the passenger is essential to smooth traffic flow at airports. More and more this will be under the control of electronic systems.

themselves as the infrastructure of tourism has enlarged and created hundreds of thousands of jobs in the new industry. Even a cursory glance at the tourist scene world-wide will reveal that this Utopian dream is far from being fulfilled.

As we have seen, the subsidiary industries of transport and accommodation which are the underpinning of the tourist industry are in dire trouble. Having developed great expectations in the growth years of the 1960s and having undertaken commitments which the then bright future seemed to underwrite, they are now fighting for survival and the problems do not concern only the transport and accommodation companies but whole countries whose economy has come to be based on tourism.

What can be done, therefore, to encourage this major world industry to thrive?

Tourism is a product just as much as a car or box of soap powder. It is something which is sold to national and foreign customers, and it earns money for hotels, transport companies and the ancilliary tourist services, as well as for all the trades that supply tourist needs, from striptease clubs to newspapers. It is therefore a negotiable item of international trade in the same way as are dairy products, cars, or other goods in which an imbalance in the import/export equation can produce adverse effects for the home industry. At present, some countries benefit considerably from the tourists of others, but perhaps, in time, the trade in tourists will be balanced out more equally between the 'export' and 'import' countries. While tourism remains a totally unregulated free enterprise system, international agreements on trade in tourists will be difficult. However, things may change.

Concorde itself may or may not survive but quite probably the future of air transport will include high fare supersonic flying and low fare mass transit super airliners.

The development of tourism in Russia is an interesting phenomenon. Today, some fifty million Russians take holidays, all of them subsidized or partly subsidized by the state in the belief that a healthy, refreshed worker produces better results than a tired one suffering from even a minor ailment. To obtain their subsidized holidays Russian workers have to show that they merit or need a holiday. The motive for taking holidays is therefore much what it was when the British took their holidays at spas, or in the early days at the seaside: one went because it was good for one's health, and, as we have seen, many employers would send their factory workers to the sea for that reason.

The Russian system permits some control of the work force in the sense that a subsidized holiday, or an incentive holiday as it is known in the West is a form of

Hundreds of millions of people each year pass through the departure gates of the world's airports, so that whatever the individual failures of airlines, the industry has an assured market.

reward; it allows control of the traffic flow to different resorts and hotels; and it makes it possible to regulate the industry because supply and demand can be controlled and investment made only when and where required. The market of fifty million people can therefore be manipulated to ensure that means of transport, hotels, restaurants and the like are fully utilized over long periods and therefore employment in the tourist areas, which includes some 2,500 doctors at spas, is maintained at a consistent level.

To the western mind such a system is, of course, unacceptable. Nevertheless it might be worth considering as an indication of the way things may develop.

In the present state of affairs it would seem that in every sphere of tourist operations there must come a collapse of the weaker elements under the economic strain and a coalescing into larger groups. In fact, as mentioned previously, this has already started taking place with numerous airlines having been absorbed into larger groups, individual hotels becoming members of a large chain, and small travel agents being acquired by larger groups. When this process reaches a level of stability it is likely that a greater compatibility will follow between the transport, accommodation, marketing and financing elements and a more integrated industry will result. It will, however, be different from the one enjoyed by the generations of middle-class tourists who patronized the Nile steamers of Thomas Cook or the luxury trains of Georges Nagelmackers and who today bemoan the fact that with over two hundred million tourists migrating all over the world there are few unspoilt villages left; but then there are few unspoilt villagers. The great invasion of tourists that has taken place over the past quarter century and the arrival of television have between them done away with the simple peasant who once touched his forelock to the tourist milords.

So it is possible that the future will see a much more regulated international tourist industry in which the relationship between affluent tourist and poor host will change, in which there will be more standardization of tourist infrastructures, and in which there will be more reciprocal trading arrangements between countries involved in the most dynamic of the world's new businesses—tourism.

Index